Studymates

25 Key Topics in Business Studies

Essential revision for coursework and examinations

Chris Sivewright

Principal, The Oxford School of Learning

www.studymates.co.uk

Other Studymates by the same author

25 Key Topics in Human Resources
25 Key Topics in Marketing

First published in 2000 by Studymates, a Division of International Briefings Ltd, Plymbridge House, Estover Road, Plymouth PL6 7PY, United Kingdom.

Telephone:	(01752) 202301
Fax:	(01752) 202333
Web site:	http://www.studymates.co.uk
Editorial email:	publisher@studymates.co.uk
Customer services:	cservs@plymbridge.com

Note: The contents of this book are offered for the purposes of general guidance only and no liability can be accepted for any loss or expense incurred as a result of relying in particular circumstances on statements made in this book. Readers are advised to check the current position with the appropriate authorities before entering into personal arrangements.

Case studies in this book are entirely fictional and any resemblance to real persons or organisations is entirely coincidental.

Typeset by PDQ Typesetting, Newcastle-under-Lyme, Staffordshire.
Printed and bound by The Cromwell Press Ltd, Trowbridge, Wiltshire.

Contents

List of illustrations

Preface

Business Studies continues to be an enormously popular area of study. The media is full of business news and features, especially in this age of increasing technical innovation, globalisation, and personal empowerment. Students enrolling on a Business Studies course today are often attracted to the field by the wide variety of topics studied. The course will typically include aspects of Marketing, Finance, Personnel and Production. Sometimes the course may be called 'Business Studies and Finance' or 'Business Studies and Marketing', thereby placing emphasis on one particular aspect of business. The Institute of Commercial Management examines students sitting for a Diploma in Business Studies, which includes examinations in Business Law, Marketing and Accounts.

It would therefore be unwise to suggest that certain topics are key to *all* Business Studies courses. There are however, a number of topics that are key to understanding the activities of business, the study of which will equip students with knowledge that may be applied to all courses. It is with this aim in mind – preparing students for *any* business course – that this book was written.

No business operates in a vacuum. The key – both for student and business manager – is to understand the relationship between the internal working of a business and the external environment in which it has to function. Often students find the economic environment the most difficult to understand and deal with in examinations. With that in mind this Studymate includes some essential chapters on inflation, unemployment and economic tools. This is *not* an Economics book as such, and the 'economics' chapters are approached from a relevant Business Studies angle. When dealing with inflation, for example, the Business Studies candidate will normally be spared a detailed knowledge of monetarism.

Continuing with the external environment theme, the book contains three chapters dealing with Europe. We could easily have included a further ten as the impact of Europe continues to grow, in both an economic and legislative sense. Trade wars over beef, compensation to Spanish fishermen and the build-up to the referendum on a single currency all ensure that Europe will dominate the political headlines.

In the case of some topics, we have started from the very beginning. This is the approached used for example in the chapters on critical path analysis and published accounts. These two areas, in particular, cause difficulties for students, and so no prior knowledge has been assumed.

25 Key Topics in Business Studies also includes two chapters dealing specifically with the central theme of Business Studies – decision-making and the interrelationship between a business and the external environment. Either of these topics could have been greatly expanded on, but this is not the primary aim of this book. The primary aim has been to include the right level of information to interest, enlighten and stimulate further thought. Business Studies is a dynamic subject, constantly changing. The practical assignments and discussion topics have been set with a view to encouraging research and further discussion.

Ideally I would have included chapters on such topics as relationship marketing, on-line shopping, Japanese business ethics and the millennium bug. However to do so would have been somewhat self-indulgent since they are not in themselves core topics to the study of Business. Nonetheless they, and other topics such as green marketing, may well be of interest to many readers, and you might well find it worth doing further research. This will not only help you make a success of your studies, but of your future career in the real world of business.

All comments on *25 Key Topics in Business Studies* are warmly welcomed and should be addressed to the author c/o the publisher (address on back cover) or forwarded by email. All correspondence will be acknowledged.

In the meantime, good luck with your studies!

Chris Sivewright
chrissivewright@studymates.co.uk

1

Using Supply and Demand Diagrams

One-minute summary – In Business Studies there are not too many diagrams to learn. One important diagram, supply and demand (more often seen in A-level Economics) can be adapted for business use. Once you have mastered this basic diagram, you can explore and expand the fundamental concept of supply and demand. In this chapter we will discuss:

▶ the basic supply and demand and equilibrium diagrams
▶ inflation diagrams
▶ taxation diagrams
▶ other areas where diagrams may be used

The basic supply and demand and equilibrium diagrams

The diagram below illustrates a demand curve. It shows how many people will buy a particular product, and how this demand changes if the customer knows that the price has risen.

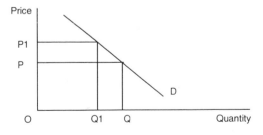

Figure 1. The demand curve.

Figure 2 shows how, if the price rises, more product is supplied to meet that demand.

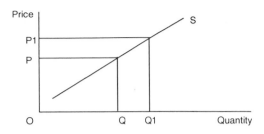

Figure 2. The supply curve.

Where demand meets supply, we have a position of equilibrium as shown below in figure 3. In this case, demand has met supply at point OP. Equilibrium is at point OP and OQ.

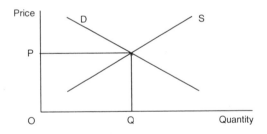

Figure 3. Demand and supply curves in equilibrium.

Inflation diagrams

Demand-pull inflation

Suppose demand increases, without a shift in the supply curve. In this case prices will rise (price inflation). How much they rise will depend on elasticity. If the demand curve shifts to the right it is known as demand-pull inflation.

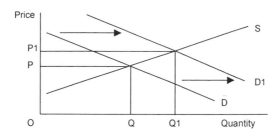

Figure 4. A demand and supply chart illustrating
demand-pull inflation.

Government has policies to control demand-pull inflation. These
policies include:

1. raising income tax
2. cutting public expenditure
3. raising interest rates (via the Bank of England in the UK).

Cost-push inflation

Figure 5 shows cost-push inflation. The supply curve shifts to the
left. This indicates a rise in costs and an unwillingness of firms to
supply goods at the previous prices. The government may
overcome this, for example by subsidising production (and so
reducing costs). This shifts the supply curve back to the right.

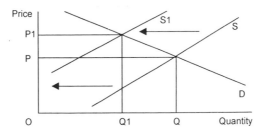

Figure 5. A demand and supply chart illustrating cost-push inflation.

Taxation diagrams

Expenditure taxation
Figure 6 shows the levying of a specific tax on a good. The two supply curves are parallel, showing that the amount of taxation does not vary according to price (unlike VAT).

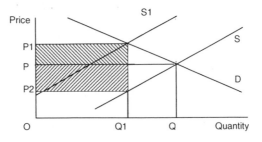

Figure 6. A supply chart illustrating the levying
of expenditure taxation.

The incidence of taxation depends on the elasticity of demand. If demand is inelastic (see next chapter) then the consumer will pay most of the tax, in other words the price increase. When the tax is levied, price rises from P to P1. The amount of tax passed on is P – P1. The amount of tax borne by the producer is P – P2. The whole tax is P2 – P1.

Value Added Tax
Figure 7 shows the levying of VAT. The supply curves are not parallel as the higher the price, the greater the taxation. At the time of writing, in the UK the VAT level is 17½%. The original price is OP. When the tax is levied the price rises to OP1, since this is the amount of tax passed onto the consumer. The tax borne by the producer is P – P2. The whole tax is P2 – P1.

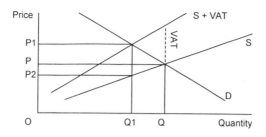

Figure 7. A supply chart showing the levying of VAT.

Other areas where diagrams may be used

Tariffs

If there is a deficit on the country's balance of payments, the government has three main choices:

► *Deflation* – Decreasing demand for products and services throughout the UK. This fall in demand will include a fall in demand for imports.

► *Devaluation* – This will cause import prices to rise and export prices to fall. A rise in import prices will cause demand to contract and fewer imports will be bought. Whether or not more is actually spent on imports than before will depend on elasticity of demand.

► *Import controls* – These include quotas, subsidies for home-produced goods, embargoes and tariffs. A tariff is a tax on the product/service.

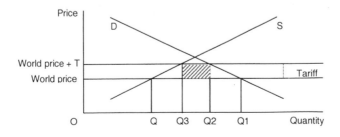

Figure 8. A demand and supply chart showing the impact of tariffs.

In figure 8 the world price is set at below the equilibrium. This means that, assuming free trade, consumers in the UK can import goods from abroad at a lower price than the domestic equilibrium. At O (world price), demand is OQ1 and domestic supply is OQ. There is thus an excess demand of Q–Q1. This is the value of imports. If the government puts a tariff on imports equivalent to:

$$(\text{world price} + \text{tariff}) - (\text{world price})$$

then the price of imported goods will rise and demand will contract.

At a higher price, domestic suppliers will supply more. Thus at O – world price + tariff, OQ2 is demanded and OQ3 is supplied (by domestic suppliers). The difference between the two – Q2–Q3, is imported. The shaded area represents the amount of tax collected by the government.

Thus the import tariff has reduced imports and raised prices at home.

The black market

A black market exists where goods and services are traded through unofficial channels. This commonly happens when prices are fixed and there is excess demand.

▶ *Example: Cup Final day* – Suppose the official price of a Cup Final ticket is £100. By the time of the Cup Final day itself, because of scarcity, the ticket may be worth far more. For example the 'going price' may be £400. The official price cannot be set at that level without public outrage over profiteering, and the long-term reputation of the suppliers being damaged. As a result, a black market is created to satisfy the demand.

In figure 9 at a price of OP, demand is OQ. Supply is OQ1. This means there is excess demand of OQ – OQ1. It is this excess demand that creates the black market.

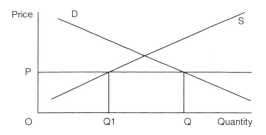

Figure 9. A demand and supply chart showing how
the black market operates.

The minimum wage

When the minimum wage was introduced into Britain, there was an outcry from employers that it would cause an explosion in wages, and that thousands of people would lose their jobs.

In figure 10 we can see the theoretical approach to the wage rise. If the market wage is OP, and a minimum wage greater than OP is imposed, the price of labour (wage) rises to OP1. At a price of OP1, demand for labour falls from OQ to OQ1. Therefore the number of people losing their jobs is OQ–OQ1.

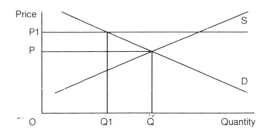

Figure 10. A demand and supply chart illustrating
the minimum wage.

The Common Agricultural Policy

In the European Union, the Common Agricultural Policy (CAP) has a number of economic features. The best known is that prices are raised above the market equilibrium in order to guarantee incomes for farmers.

In figure 11 we see that price is above the equilibrium. The new supply curve is PRTS. At that price there is excess supply of RT. It is this excess supply that creates the butter mountains, wine lakes and other commodity surpluses that are widely reported in the media.

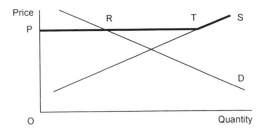

Figure 11. A demand and supply chart showing how the Common Agricultural Policy creates butter mountains.

Exchange rates
It is important for you as a student to be able to manipulate the demand and supply curves. In figure 12 we see shifts in demand and supply of currency. (The causes and impact of changes in the exchange rate are discussed thoroughly in chapter 7.) A shift of the demand curve to the right is an increase in demand; a shift of the supply curve to the left is a decrease in supply.

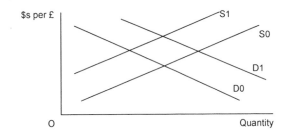

Figure 12. A demand and supply chart illustrating how the exchange rate works.

If the demand for currency rises (disregarding speculation) this represents an increase in demand for exports. This will cause the exchange rate to rise. If the supply curve shifts to the left, this represents a *fall* in the demand for imports, as sterling is supplied in order to buy foreign currency, to buy imports.

Where demand and supply meet, there is equilibrium. Thus we can use this diagram to show the impact on exchange rates of a rise/fall in demand for imports/exports.

Tutorial: helping you learn

Progress questions

1. Draw the diagram that illustrates the levying of VAT. Clearly show which part of the tax the consumer pays and which part the producer pays.

2. With reference to question 1, explain the impact of elasticity on the amount of tax passed on to the consumer.

Discussion point

Why might businesses fear a high rate of inflation?

Practical assignment

Go through your syllabus and see how you could use basic supply and demand graphs to illustrate those areas. One example would be the exchange rate mechanism.

Study/revision tip

If the demand or supply curve shifts to the right that is an increase; to the left it is a decrease. The point where demand and supply meet is called equilibrium.

2

Elasticity

One-minute summary – The concept of elasticity runs all through the Business Studies syllabus. In business terms, elasticity means responsiveness, and the successful business is the one that responds to change. There are five main types of elasticity, each showing the response of one variable to another. All elasticities assume *ceteris paribus* 'all things being equal'. This assumption means that decisions based on elasticity alone are at best risky and, at worst, foolhardy. In this chapter we will discuss:

▶ elasticity – the concept
▶ degrees of elasticity
▶ the major types of elasticity
▶ factors affecting elasticity of demand
▶ elasticity applied

Elasticity – the concept

'Elasticity' means responsiveness. For example:

▶ *price elasticity of demand* – measures how demand responds to a change in price.

▶ *income elasticity of demand* – measures how demand responds to a change in income.

Degrees of elasticity

Demand may be elastic, inelastic, perfectly inelastic, perfectly elastic or unit elastic. If the degree of responsiveness (elasticity) is greater than 1, then demand is said to be elastic. If the responsiveness is between 0 and 1 then demand is said to be inelastic.

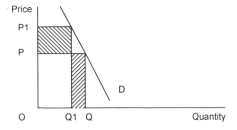

Figure 13. Inelastic demand.

Figure 13 above shows inelastic demand. If price is raised from P to P1 then demand falls from OQ to OQ1. From this diagram we can clearly see that a large price rise leads to a smaller quantity fall. The price rise will therefore lead to an increase in total revenue.

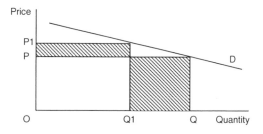

Figure 14. Elastic demand.

Figure 14 shows elastic demand. If the price is raised from P to P1, then demand falls from OQ to OQ1. The fall in quantity demanded is greater than the price rise. In this example, the retailer would lose if he raised the price.

In each case the shaded area shows the amount of gain and loss.

Factors affecting elasticity of demand

1. Whether there are substitutes for the product. If there are, then

a price rise in the product is likely to lead to an increase in demand for the other product.

2. What proportion of income is spent on the product. For example, say a box of matches costs 10p. If the price doubles, most people can still afford the box and so demand will hardly change.

3. Whether the product is a necessity. The greater the need for the product, the less responsive demand will be to a price change.

4. The degree of addiction – if any – to the product. Cigarette smokers are often addicted to the nicotine in the cigarettes. Thus if prices are raised, demand will hardly change.

The major types of elasticity

Price elasticity of demand
Price elasticity of demand is measured by application of the following formula:

$$\text{price elasticity of demand} = \frac{\% \text{ change in quantity demanded}}{\% \text{ change in price}}$$

Suppose that the price of a product falls from 20p to 15p (a fall of 25%), and that the demand is observed to rise from 100 units to 200 units (a rise of 100%). Elasticity of demand would be calculated like this:

$$\frac{\% \text{ change in quantity of demand}}{\% \text{ change in price}} = \frac{100\%}{= -25\%}$$

This gives us a measurement of -4. (Note: With price elasticity of demand, the positive or negative sign is ignored, since it is simply the *degree* of responsiveness that we wish to measure.)

Demand for most goods rises when price falls, and falls when price rises. Exceptions are very expensive goods bought in part because they *are* expensive, a form of consumer behaviour known as 'conspicuous consumption'.

Income elasticity of demand

This measures the responsiveness of demand to a change in income. The formula is:

$$\frac{\% \text{ change in quantity demanded}}{\% \text{ change in income}}$$

The greater the value, the more elastic is the demand (to a change in income). This has particular significance to retailers when the government cuts direct taxes and so increases disposable income (income after tax).

If the reaction is negative (incomes rise, but demand falls), the good is deemed inferior or a substitute. If a consumer normally buys a cheaper brand of butter owing to costs, and his income rises, it is likely the consumer will shift to the better quality butter.

Cross elasticity of demand

This measures how the price change of one good affects the demand for another. The formula is:

$$\frac{\% \text{ change in quantity demanded of one good (eg 'good A')}}{\% \text{ change in price of another good (eg 'good B')}}$$

If the result is positive (the price rise in one good leads to an increase in quantity demanded of the other good) then the two goods are substitutes. The greater the numerical elasticity the greater the degree of substitution.

If the cross-elasticity is negative, then the goods are complements. For example, if car prices rise, there is less demand for petrol.

Advertising elasticity of demand

This measures how demand responds to a change in advertising expenditure. The greater the response of demand, the more effective advertising would seem to be. The formula is:

$$\frac{\% \text{ change in quantity demanded}}{\% \text{ change in advertising expenditure}}$$

Elasticity of supply

This measures the responsiveness of supply to a change in price. In the figure 15 we can see that, if price changes from P to P1, then supply will extend, in other words from Q to Q1. Where the supply line goes towards the vertical axis, the supply is elastic.

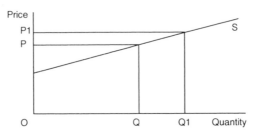

Figure 15. Elastic supply.

In figure 16, supply is inelastic. The supply curve is going through the horizontal axis. If price rises from P to P1 then supply extends by less, in other words from Q to Q1.

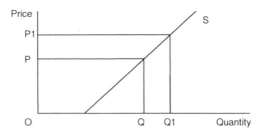

Figure 16. Inelastic supply.

Factors affecting elasticity of supply

1. The length of time it takes to produce the product.

2. The level of stocks of the product – the greater the stock level, the more quickly the retailer can react to a sudden surge in demand for the product.

3. The availability and the mobility of resources used in production.

4. Weather for example, a favourable climate helps crops to grow.

5. External factors – for example the level of employment. If labour is in short supply then it will be harder to increase production quickly.

Elasticity applied

We can apply the concept of elasticity to all kinds of situations. Remember, elasticity assumes that nothing else changes beyond the two items in the formula. This means that if price falls, and more goods are demanded, then we are assuming that this change in demand is a result of the fall alone; we are assuming that nothing else changes. In reality, there could be other factors at work – changes in taste, fashion, a price drop by competitors, or an advertising campaign finally bearing fruit.

We will now give a very brief outline of the application of elasticity.

Elasticity and wages
Price elasticity of demand – can workers raise their wages? People work for money. That is the price of labour. Thus demand for a worker may be inelastic. In other words, if the worker puts up his price (his wages), then demand for his services may not fall if it is difficult to replace that worker.

Elasticity and sales revenue
If a business drops the price of one of its products, and demand is elastic, sales revenue will rise. However, profits may fall if the price is dropped so low that variable costs are barely covered.

Elasticity and stock levels
The elasticity of supply will affect how long it takes to deliver the goods in time to meet the order.

The balance of payments

The balance of payments is affected by the level of imports and exports. If the exchange rate falls, exports will become cheaper and imports more expensive. How demand reacts to these two changes will determine the outcome in terms of revenue for the balance of payments.

Income tax cuts

This will lead to shops selling goods at the luxury end of the market experiencing a rise in demand.

Tutorial: helping you learn

Progress test

1. Outline the formula for cross-elasticity of demand. Assess why the results may change.

2. State two factors affecting:

   (a) elasticity of demand
   (b) elasticity of supply

Discussion point

The diagram below shows the supply of the pound. From the diagram, can you tell whether the demand for imports is elastic or inelastic? (Remember, you sell pounds to buy foreign goods.)

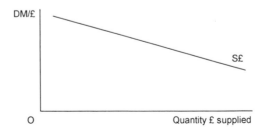

Figure 17. Supply of the pound.

Practical assignments

1. List the prices of ten products from your local supermarket. Decide which ones are elastic in supply and which ones are inelastic in supply. What factors affect this elasticity?

2. When choosing a product, the greater the variety of choice, the more elastic demand becomes; not only the existence of choice but the methods of purchase will make a difference. Go to:

   http://news2.thls.bbc.co.uk/hi/english/uk/newsid%5F610000/
   610280.stm

and consider the impact that online availability has on demand for the product. In what ways may an attractive, eye-catching web page actually make demand for that product inelastic? Evaluate the effect the Competition Commission is having on competition in the marketplace. For further information go to:

   http://www.mmc.gov.uk/

Study tip/revision point

Elasticity measures responsiveness of one factor to another. With the above formula always remember that the calculation assumes no change in other possible variables!

3

Inflation

One-minute summary - In recent years, inflation in the UK has been falling. In 1988 inflation was 4.9%. It rose to 9.5% in 1990, but by 1999 it had fallen back to 1.3% There are different ways of measuring inflation, and different policies a government may use in trying to reduce it. To some extent those policies will depend on the causes of inflation – about which there is often argument. Whichever approach is used, there will be an impact on businesses. In this chapter we will discuss:

▶ definitions of inflation
▶ causes of inflation
▶ controlling inflation in the short term
▶ controlling inflation in the long term
▶ the impact of inflation on a business

Definitions of inflation

There are several definitions for inflation, and the choice of definition depends on exactly which category is being measured.

▶ *Basic definition* – Inflation is a sustained increase in the general price level.

Inflation is measured by the Retail Price Index (RPI). The index shows the annual price changes of 600 different goods and services. A total of some 150,000 price quotations are taken each month, and the average price calculated for each product. The items in the index are weighted to represent their relative importance in the family budget.

RPIX

Also called 'underlying inflation', this index measures RPI excluding mortgage payments, with the 'X' representing that exclusion. This measurement began in the late 1980s when the anti-inflation strategy of the government was based on high interest rates. It is the RPIX that is the government's target rate both then and now.

RPIY

By removing indirect taxes from inflation calculations, governments may raise one of them (say VAT) without raising inflation. This measurement therefore comprises RPIX (described above) less council tax, duties, VAT, car purchase tax, airport tax, insurance tax and vehicle excise duty.

Causes of inflation

Excess demand in the economy (demand-pull inflation)

If aggregate demand exceeds aggregate supply, prices will rise. The nearer an economy approaches full employment, the less spare capacity there will be. As capacity utilisation moves close to 100% the lack of spare resources will cause shortages and bottlenecks, increasing inflationary pressure still further.

Cost-push inflation

When costs rise for a firm, that firm is likely to increase price, not least to protect its profit margin. The rise in costs will be caused by one or more of the following:

1. A rise in input costs – perhaps a fall in the exchange rate has made imported supplies more expensive. (See chapter 7 on exchange rates for more about factors affecting exchange rates, and the impact of exchange rate fluctuations.)

2. Growth in labour costs resulting from wage rises, shortfalls in productivity or changes in legislation.

3. Increases in indirect taxes, which adds a tax onto some goods and services. This price increase is then passed on, in whole or part, to the consumer.

Monetary inflation

Monetarists maintain that when the money supply increases, there will be inflation some 12 to 18 months later. However, there are different definitions of the money supply. For the purposes of this chapter, we will take 'money supply' to represent notes and coins in circulation plus money in credit and deposit accounts in banks. Monetary inflation is caused by individuals spending excess money balances, causing an increase in demand for labour, a rise in wages – and further inflation.

Controlling inflation in the short term

Government short-term policies are usually aimed at reducing demand. If demand falls then wages are likely to stop rising. This is because the demand for labour is derived from the demand for goods. Equally, the prices of goods and services should fall, as firms start dropping prices in order to sell their goods. There are various ways in which demand may be reduced: monetary policy, fiscal policy and wage controls.

Monetary policy

Until the Labour government came to power in 1997, the control of interest rates lay with the government. Since 1997, however, interest rates have been set by a Monetary Policy Committee which advises the Bank of England. If interest rates are raised:

1. Borrowing – and thus demand – will decrease.

2. Savings will increase, meaning less money is spent on consumption.

3. Mortgages will rise. Consumers will have less discretionary income available for expenditure

Fiscal policy

Direct taxes may be raised. This will reduce disposable income and hence demand. Also, public sector expenditure may be cut, further reducing demand as some people in government and local authorities lose their jobs.

Wage controls

The government could introduce an 'incomes policy'. The aim would be to reduce or cancel wage claims in the economy. In the 1980s and 1990s wages in the private sector became difficult to control, so governments tried to control public sector pay instead. They hoped, by setting a good example, that private sector pay rises would match those in the public sector.

Controlling inflation in the long term

'Supply-side policies' are those aimed at increasing aggregate supply in the economy. As output increases, then supply will increase and prices will fall. Policies to increase supply or reduce the costs of supplying include:

1. a drop in interest rates to encourage investment
2. a drop in income tax to encourage unemployed people to look for work
3. policies to improve competition, since competition tends to reduce costs
4. policies to improve productivity, including funding for education, training and research.

The impact of inflation on a business

Inflation reduces the ability to compete in the global market

If inflation is higher in the UK than in other states, the UK will lose its ability to compete internationally. The excess demand will also lead to a rise in imports and a worsening trade deficit. Assuming a floating exchange rate, the pound will fall. This will make import prices more expensive – and inflation even worse.

Inflation encourages a wage price spiral

Inflation may also encourage workers to press for a pay increase. If granted, that pay increase may lead to another, which will then lead to inflation – and yet another pay increase.

Inflation reduces the value of debtors

Inflation will reduce the true value of a firm's debtors (the money owed to a business). The value will fall 'in real terms', that is, when taking inflation into account.

Inflation engenders uncertainty

Just as the value of debtors may change, so will the value of fixed assets, stock and profits. Revenue may rise, not because of rising sales volume but because of rising prices. Suppose that sales revenue rises by 4% in an economic climate where inflation is 7%. In real terms, sales have fallen in value by 3%. Budgeting, in particular, becomes a problem as expenses soar.

Inflation increases the cost of production

If interest rates are raised, a firm that borrows money will have to pay more to the lender. This increases the overall cost of producing goods just when the firm is unable to increase prices because of reduced demand.

The reduced demand may cause the firm to make redundancies; the resulting lowering of morale may cause a reduction in productivity, thereby increasing unit labour costs.

Inflation reduces profit margins

As demand for products fall, the firm may cut its prices and therefore reduce its profit margins.

Tutorial: helping you learn

Progress questions

1. Define RPIX and RPIY.

2. How is inflation calculated?

3. Who loses when there is inflation – debtors or creditors?

Discussion point

In 1997, a Labour government replaced a Conservative one, which had been in office for 18 years. At the 1999 Labour party conference, the Labour chancellor said:

> 'And it is because we rejected not just the Tory policy but the flawed Tory values behind it – their short-termist, take-what-you-can, selfish irresponsibility – and it is because we put in their place Labour values of economic responsibility, planning for the long term, building stability from solid foundations - that we now in our country have mortgage rates around their lowest levels for twenty years, inflation at its lowest level in over thirty years, long term interest rates at their lowest levels in nearly 40 years and not just one hundred thousand additional jobs or 200,000 additional jobs but today in Britain, 648,000 more jobs, more people in work – over 27 million men and women – than ever before in our history.'

How much of the credit for this – if any – can be claimed by the Labour government?

Practical assignment

Research the figures for inflation, the money supply and the personal savings ratio. The personal savings ratio is the relationship between savings and disposable income after tax of individuals. The theory is that as interest rates rise, the savings ratio will rise due to people wishing to capitalise on the higher rate of return. Plot the three sets of figures on a single graph. Are you able to draw any conclusions?

Study/revision tip

Inflation is usually caused by excess demand – somewhere. Perhaps the demand for labour is too high, causing wages to rise. Perhaps there is an excess demand for goods, causing demand to rise. Policies to overcome inflation will cause demand to fall, and this will have a number of effects on a firm. Think of the effects in terms of departments; in other words, consider how will a fall in demand will affect Personnel, Marketing, Finance and Production.

4

Unemployment

One-minute summary – Unemployment is a waste of resources. The cost of unemployment may be calculated as the costs of social security benefits, or the costs of benefits plus the costs of taxes lost, or as just as a percentage of output. Suppose that 90% of the working population creates £450bn worth of output, and that unemployment is 10%. If unemployment were zero, output would be £500bn. Unemployment has different effects on a firm as people are recruited (supply) and as people buy goods (demand). Thus high unemployment means more labour is supplied – but equally demand for the product may fall owing to a fall in incomes. In this chapter we will discuss:

▶ the definition of unemployment
▶ types of unemployment and their causes
▶ solutions for unemployment
▶ the costs of unemployment
▶ the impact of unemployment

The definition of unemployment

Unemployment – in terms of government statistics and eligibility for benefits – refers to those who are registered as able, available and willing to work at the going wage rate in any suitable job. They must be looking for work (and able to prove this) but unable to find it. (Note: there is often disagreement as to what is a 'suitable' job.)

Types of unemployment and their causes

Classical unemployment
This is also called 'real wage' unemployment. It is caused by

workers or trade unions forcing employers to pay higher wages:

1. without justifying the increase with a corresponding increase in productivity

2. without the increased wages causing an increase in demand for products to offset the resulting unemployment.

Demand-deficient unemployment
This is unemployment caused by lack of demand. In a recession (defined as 'two consecutive quarters of negative economic growth') demand for products will be low – and so demand for labour will be low. Unemployed people have low incomes and so a rise in unemployment will further depress demand and cause even more unemployment.

Frictional unemployment
This category refers to workers who are between jobs. Owing to lack of information, they cannot immediately find new work. Policies to reduce this type of unemployment include:

1. cutting income tax to incentivise the unemployed by allowing them to keep a larger proportion of future earnings

2. increasing the amount of job information, such as on teletext and on 24-hour terminals outside public libraries.

Structural unemployment
This refers to unemployment caused by the decline of an industry. When workers are made redundant, they will need time to learn the skills needed to increase their occupational mobility.

Solutions for unemployment

Demand side policies
Demand side policies consist of stimulating demand for products in the economy. This may include increasing government expenditure, especially on labour-intensive industries.

In 1998-99, the Labour government paid out around £100bn on social security. If unemployment could be reduced, this spending in particular would fall. Other policies to reduce demand-deficient unemployment include:

1. cutting income tax to increase disposable income

2. dropping interest rates to encourage borrowing and hence more spending

3. devaluing the pound, causing the exchange rate to fall. Exports become cheaper and more attractive abroad. The problem with this policy is that imports rise in price and, unless there are substitutes at home, this is likely to cause inflation.

Supply side policies
Supply side policies include:

1. privatisation – as a means of making industry more competitive, and therefore willing to employ more people as the business expands

2. reform of the trade unions – thus reducing one of the barriers to employment and one of the forces for wage increases

3. direct tax cuts – making it worthwhile for unemployed people to look for work

4. improved job information – in particular through the internet.

The 'New Deal' is one of the Labour government's main policies to reduce unemployment. It was launched in 1998 and employers were given job subsidies to take on unemployed workers. The Labour government *Annual Report 1998/99* states:

> 'The government is helping people into work through the New Deal ... and by making work pay through the Working Families Tax Credit and the new national minimum wage...'

At the time of writing (late 1999), 27.34 million people are in employment in the UK. This is 1.5% more than in 1998. Around 12.25 million of them are women, and 15.09 million men. In the March 1999 budget the chancellor said (about the New Deal):

'Most fundamentally the tax reforms of this budget provide a better deal for the hard working majority – a ladder of opportunity for those who want to work their way up, a chance to keep more of what they earn and, for all, a fundamental guarantee that work will pay ... 230,000 young people are already benefiting from the New Deal. ... This will be our New Deal for 1999: better provision but tougher conditions. Our responsibility is to offer training and intensive coaching. In return their responsibility is to come into the New Deal, get the skills and prepare to take up a job.'

The impact of unemployment

The impact on workers, the economy and the local community
Unemployment represents a waste of scarce resources. Unemployed people receive benefit, and contribute no income tax. Also, because of their fall in spending power, they contribute less to the government through buying goods subject to indirect taxation.

An unemployed worker produces no output directly, though of course his or her limited spending power makes up an element of the aggregate demand curve.

The longer workers are out of work, the more difficult it is to find work, since their skills may be out of date.

As unemployment continues, so crime rises and social deprivation gets worse.

The impact on a business
With high unemployment, incomes fall. If a business stocks goods aimed at the upper levels of the market, its sales may fall dramatically as peoples' incomes fall. With this fall in demand may come a cash flow problem and a shortening of the product life cycle. New product developments will be shelved and investment

projects cancelled. Workers may be made redundant, worsening the situation, and trade unions will strive to protect the remaining employees.

Tutorial: helping you learn

Progress questions

1. Who are the 'unemployed'?

2. Outline Labour's 'New Deal'.

3. What is demand-deficient unemployment?

Discussion point

Which are more effective in reducing unemployment: supply side or demand side policies?

Practical assignment

Research the types of unemployment and policies not covered in this chapter, in particular voluntary unemployment, and technological unemployment. Would the policies to reduce these two categories be the same as the national policies?

Study/revision tip

To overcome unemployment, you stimulate demand. If demand is over-stimulated the result is inflation. The government thus operates rather like a valve, creating a little more demand here, a little less demand there, and so on.

5

Economic Growth

One-minute summary – If demand in the economy is increasing then demand for a business's goods or services will also increase. Equally if demand is falling, so will the demand for the goods or services produced by business. In between the rise and the fall there may also be a period of stability. All three of these situations will have an impact on business – both long and short term. The impact will not just be on profits, but also on the people who work there and the people who invest, in other words on all those with an interest in the business. These are the 'stakeholders' in a business. The business may take steps to maximise/minimise the effects of the growth/recession. No business acts in isolation, so these steps – and those taken by the government and Bank of England – will also have effects. In this chapter we will discuss:

▶ economic growth
▶ long-term economic growth
▶ the business cycle
▶ government policy and economic growth
▶ specific policies to stimulate economic growth

Economic growth

There are two types of economic growth:

▶ *actual growth* – The rate of growth of actual output measured in terms of gross domestic product (GDP) or gross national product (GNP).

▶ *potential growth* – The percentage annual increase in the capacity to grow, in other words the economy's capacity to produce.

43

If the potential growth rate exceeds the actual growth rate, then capacity will exceed actual output. The greater this gap – between actual and potential – the greater will be the unemployment level.

'The government's central economic objective is to achieve high and stable levels of economic growth and employment so that everyone can share higher living standards and greater job opportunities'. (Source: Treasury Statement 1997.)

Lack of growth and lack of higher living standards are believed to have been behind the military coup in Pakistan in October 1999.

Long-term economic growth

This is determined by the following factors:

Technological progress
The faster the progress, the greater the economic growth. Technology will increase the productivity of capital.

The workforce
This includes the output per worker. This will be influenced by education and training, by skills already acquired, and by health.

Market forces
The degree of competition within markets will affect long-term economic growth. This applies both to the products being sold and to the human factors being recruited to make the products.

External factors
The most important external factors that will come into play are:

1. inflation, because it will affect the international competitiveness of goods sold overseas
2. unemployment, because it will affect demand for the goods as well as the supply of labour to produce those goods.

Innovation
This refers to the commercial applications of invention.

The business cycle

The business cycle is also known as the 'trade cycle'. There are four stages of the cycle as illustrated in figure 18.

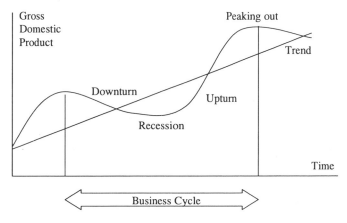

Figure 18. The business cycle.

The various stages of the business cycle described below may vary in length and from cycle to cycle. A recession may last for three months – or several years. To some extent government policy will influence growth.

Stage 1 – the upturn
A recession is defined as the growth stage where there have been two consecutive periods of negative economic growth. With an upturn the economy is moving out of the lowest point of the recession and there is growth in actual output. In such conditions, a firm might:

(a) move part-time workers to full-time
(b) employ more workers
(c) increase output in anticipation of increased demand
(d) build up stock
(e) borrow more funds to invest in machinery

(f) consider launching a new product

(g) raise prices.

Stage 2 – the boom

In this phase of the business cycle, the rate of economic growth increases. More resources are used. Actual and potential outputs converge. In such conditions a firm might:

(a) raise prices

(b) launch complementary products

(c) issue shares

(d) seek new distributors to speed up and widen distribution

(e) agree pay rises to prevent a strike so that sales may be maximised

(f) advertise to inform rather than persuade.

Stage 3 – peaking out

This is the highest point of the cycle. The rate of growth slows, possibly stopping altogether. In such conditions a firm might:

(a) cease extra recruitment

(b) put all pay negotiations on 'hold'

(c) reconsider the launching of new products

(d) cut back on borrowing

(e) give customers less credit

(f) postpone consideration of long-term investment projects.

Stage 4 – recession

Growth is now in the negative stage. There is increasing slack in the economy. Unemployment rises. In such conditions a firm might:

(a) look for markets overseas

(b) make workers redundant

(c) try to cut wages, or at least resist further pay increases

(d) borrow to survive

(e) consider merging to survive

(f) rationalise production

(g) distance the corporate image from declining brands
(h) lease business assets (buildings, plant, vehicles) rather than buy
    them.

Government policy and economic growth

Given that the aim of government is to have economic growth, it
can be seen from the following chart that there was a recession in
the UK in 1991. According to a report from the National
Westminster Bank, 69% of total GDP growth between 1992 and
1997 was due to consumption, 12% to capital investment and 9%
to net external trade.

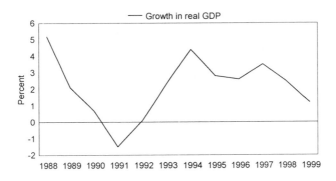

Figure 19. The growth in real GDP between 1988 and 1999.

Clearly there are factors that affect growth, and government
policy can affect those factors. The key factor that the government
can influence is aggregate demand. In a boom, aggregate demand
rises. The speed of the rise is thus the rate of economic growth. A
recession occurs when aggregate demand has fallen.

Aggregate demand
Aggregate demand is the total spending on goods and services
made within one country. 'Total spending' consists of:

1. consumer spending – influenced by income, interest rates,
   consumer confidence, and credit arrangements

2. investment by firms – influenced by business confidence, government investment, and interest rates
3. government spending – on health, defence and education and other areas
4. exports – net of imports. Exports are affected by the exchange rate, world confidence/opinion and steps by producers/government to encourage overseas trade.

Specific government policies to stimulate growth

Policies may be aimed at the demand side and/or the supply side of the economy. If there is enough demand, then firms will invest and potential output is realised.

Equally – and not exclusively – policies may be aimed at increasing the supply side of the economy. These would be measures to ensure that the market worked better and that potential output increased. Thus policies to increase growth may include:

1. Tax-cuts to stimulate demand, and also to encourage unemployed people to apply for jobs. The tax rate fall means that a greater proportion of gross earnings would be kept by the worker.

2. Devaluation which will lead to exports falling in price (leading to a rise in demand) and imports rising in price (leading to a fall in demand).

3. Increasing government investment – thus encouraging other firms to invest too.

4. A dropping of interest rates (by the Bank of England) to encourage firms to invest and consumers to borrow (and spend).

The effect on a firm of policies to stimulate growth is that there will be an increase in demand for the goods and services sold. The degree of increase depends on income elasticity of demand. As demand grows so must supply. However, the firm may also be experiencing labour shortage problems and wages may have to be increased to attract the extra employees needed.

In short, economic growth will usually lead to higher profits for individual firms so long as actual output does not exceed potential. If potential is exceeded (that is, if capacity does not meet demand) there is likely to be inflation.

Tutorial: helping you learn

Progress questions
1. Define 'economic growth'.

2. What is the difference between 'actual' and 'potential' growth?

3. How would a fall in interest rates affect economic growth?

4. What are the stages of the business cycle?

Discussion points
1. Is economic growth always desirable?

2. Why might a high rate of economic growth also cause inflation?

Practical assignment
Go to the following discussion on the internet. Is there a case against increasing economic growth? Support your answer with information from other web sites.

http://www.stanford.edu/~promer/Econgro.htm

Study/revision tip
To increase economic growth injections into the economy, we need to increase: government spending, exports and investment. Additionally withdrawals can be reduced: savings, tax and imports.

6

Balance of Payments

One-minute summary A Balance of Payments is a kind of a balance sheet between one country and the rest of the world. It has two main component parts – the capital account and the current account. Generally, if imports exceed exports then there will be a deficit, if not on the entire balance of payments then at least on the balance of trade. A deficit may be overcome through devaluation, deflation and/or import controls. All three of these policies will impact on the firm, depending on whether it is an importer, exporter or both. In this chapter we will discuss:

▶ Balance of Payments defined
▶ causes of a current account deficit
▶ policies to overcome a Balance of Payments deficit
▶ impact of such policies on a firm
▶ import and export growth

Balance of Payments defined

The Balance of Payments is a record of all the financial transactions between one country (for example the UK) and the rest of the world. It is *not* just a record of government transactions, but the transactions of *all* firms and individuals as well as the government, and the rest of the world. Thus one firm may import cars and another firm may export them.

The Balance of Payments is split into two accounts:

▶ *The current account* – records the trade in goods and services

▶ *The capital account* – records capital flows between the UK and the rest of the world

Causes of a deficit in the current account

A deficit on the current account means that more money is leaving the UK through expenditure on imported goods and services than is coming in. This could be because of a net import of goods, of services, or both.

The overall reason is a lack of international competitiveness. This could be because exports are not competitive enough, domestic goods are not as attractive as imports, or both. The reasons behind this lack of competitiveness include:

1. Too high a price – possibly caused by a high exchange rate which makes imported goods cheap and exported goods more expensive.

2. High labour costs owing to high wages, low productivity, or both.

3. Poor product design.

4. Late delivery of goods as a result of inelastic supply. In a recession, for example, factories close and people are made redundant; if there is then a sudden increase in domestic demand it is likely to be met through greater imports rather than home production. Disused factories cannot suddenly be kick-started back into life; unemployed workers cannot quickly be moved and retrained to meet demand.

More about the capital account

The capital account includes the liabilities of UK to residents of other countries. The more inward investment is encouraged, the more UK assets will be owned by overseas interests. If the UK stays outside of the European single currency, it is likely to lead to less inward investment. The capital account may move into surplus and so reduce the Balance of Payments deficit on current account.

Policies to overcome a Balance of Payments deficit

There are three main methods to overcome a deficit on the Balance of Payments: deflation, devaluation, and import controls.

Devaluation

If the pound is devalued, then less foreign currency may be purchased with UK currency. Suppose a good previously cost $10, where £1 = $2, and the currency is then devalued by 10%. £1 will now only be worth $1.80. Assuming no price change in dollars, the good will now cost £5.55 ($10/$1.80) instead of £5 ($10/$2).

Equally, goods sold overseas will fall in price. If the price was previously £5 ($10) it will now be $9 (£5 x $1.80). Whether or not the UK gains from such a devaluation will depend on the following factors:

1. Elasticity of demand for imports – if demand is inelastic then spending on imports may actually increase.

2. Elasticity of demand for exports – if price falls then the response of demand to the price fall will determine how much extra revenue is raised.

3. The elasticity of supply, as if demand for imports falls, and exports rises, there must be enough domestic supply to meet the changes.

Deflation

The government may slow down growth in the economy, for example through cutting government expenditure, raising taxes, or by the Bank of England raising interest rates. In this case, less goods – both imports and home produced goods – will be bought. This slowdown in imports (assuming no change in exports) will reduce the deficit because less money will leave the country.

Import controls

There are a variety of import controls. The main two are tariffs (taxes on imports) and quotas (numerical restrictions on imports). If fewer imports come in, or if prices rise (owing to the tariff) causing demand to contract, demand for home-produced goods will rise.

The downside is that some of the imported goods may be far better quality than those at home, and so consumers will lose out.

Impact of such policies on firms

If demand throughout the economy slows (deflation) then individual firms will suffer. The fall in demand will affect their own profits, cash flow and sales revenues. This may in turn lead to redundancies and a decision by firms to reduce the number of products available. Development of new products may be restricted.

If tariffs are imposed on imported goods then their price will rise (unless firms overseas absorb the tariff and reduce their prices). This will increase the importing firms' costs. Passing these costs on to consumers, will cause cost-push inflation.

If the firm is a competitor of importers, then the tariff will decrease the competitiveness of the importing firms. In this case the domestic non-importer may gain and recruit, increase production and expand.

With devaluation, where import prices rise and export prices fall, the exporter will find it easier to sell his products but the importer will find it more expensive to acquire the goods. If the exporter is able to increase production to meet the increase in demand (owing to the price fall) then profits will increase. However, the same firm may also be importing. In this case the change in profits will depend on which goods are imported (and the volume) and which goods are exported.

Import and export growth

In the UK, imports have grown faster than exports in recent years.

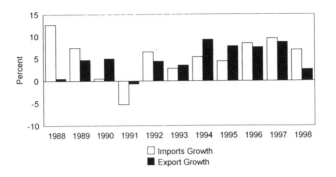

Figure 20. The growth in imports and exports.

The volume of imports may grow when domestic goods are not competitive enough, as explained above. Another reason could be that demand for imports tends to be income-elastic. In other words, as incomes rise, so does demand. Thus if the UK experiences a higher rate of growth than other nations, demand for exports is likely to fall (as incomes abroad fall) but demand for imports will rise. Thus, in the short term, a trade deficit is not necessarily a sign that a country is doing badly.

Tutorial: helping you learn

Progress questions
1. If the pound falls, do export prices rise or fall?

2. Why might the government want to restrict imports?

3. What does deflation mean?

4. What is included in the Balance of Payments?

Discussion point
Does the current account deficit matter, or could it simply be a necessary evil of a growing economy?

Practical assignments

1. Research the figures for the UK Balance of Payments for the years 1988 to 2000. Plot the figures on a graph and suggest reasons for the changes in deficit and surpluses. Can the balance of payments figures be linked to economic growth? The Treasury web site on the internet could be of help:

   http://www.hm-treasury.gov.uk

2. 'The gap in performance between UK manufacturing and service industries narrowed in the third quarter of the year, according to official data.

   'Figures for gross domestic product (GDP), which measures economic growth, showed manufacturing growing faster than services for the first time since the second quarter of 1995. Service business grew by 0.6% in the three months to September, according to data from the Office for National Statistics (ONS). This was lower than previous estimates of 0.9%.

   'At the same time, manufacturing output rose by 1.2%, driven by strong growth in the electrical equipment and chemicals industries.' Source: *BBC Online 22.12.99*.

   (a) How may a strong pound affect the Balance of Payments?

   (b) If the UK is growing faster than other European countries, is this likely to create a Balance of Payments surplus or deficit?

   (c) Research the main components in the Balance of Payments and chart their growth/decline over a period of months.

Study/revision tip

If the Balance of Payments is in deficit, this is *usually* because more is spent on imports than is received for exports.

7

Exchange Rates

One-minute summary An exchange rate is the value of one currency in terms of another. As the exchange rate rises, so does the price of exports. The effect of this on the exporter depends partly on the elasticity of demand. The effect it has on the economy depends on the number of firms importing, exporting, and competing with importers. To measure the effects of changes in the exchange rate, we can think of the impact on a firm (microeconomics) as well as the impact on the economy (macroeconomics). Exchange rate movements may be depicted using supply and demand diagrams. In this chapter we will discuss:

▶ the definition of exchange rate
▶ factors affecting an exchange rate
▶ factors in the economy that affect the demand for imports/ exports
▶ the effect of exchange rate movements on a firm
▶ the effect of exchange rate movements on the economy

The definition of exchange rate

According to *A Dictionary of Economics and Commerce* (ISBN 0 330 24552 X) an exchange rate is 'The price at which one currency can be exchanged for another, *i.e.* the price of a currency in the foreign exchange market'.

Figure 21 illustrates the exchange rate of sterling in terms of US dollars. Equilibrium of demand and supply is at a rate of exchange of $1.60 = £1. In order to look at exchange rate movements, we must consider factors affecting the demand and supply of a currency.

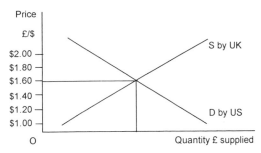

Figure 21. Exchange rate of sterling against the dollar.

Factors affecting an exchange rate

Factors affecting demand for a currency
The diagram above shows the exchange rate of sterling against the dollar, but it could just as easily show any other two currencies in the world, for example the yen against the deutschmark. Similarly, the factors affecting the demand for a currency apply to any currency in the world. These factors include:

1. export of goods
2. exports of services
3. inflows of direct investment
4. inflows of portfolio investment
5. speculative demand
6. intervention by the central bank where it buys up the native currency.

Using the sterling/dollar example again, when people or businesses in the United States buy the UK's exports, they have to pay in sterling. Therefore, if exports rise in volume, so will demand for sterling, and the demand curve will shift to the right. If this happens then the 'price' (the exchange rate) of sterling will rise, assuming there are no other changes.

Factors affecting the supply of sterling
These are the direct opposite of the factors affecting demand listed above. In other words, they include the imports of goods instead of

exports of goods, speculative selling instead of speculative buying, and selling of the native currency rather than buying.

We now have an outline of the main factors affecting the exchange rate, in other words the demand and supply of currency. We must next look at the factors affecting the demand for exports and imports in order to fully understand exchange rates. For this we can look at events in the economy.

Factors in the economy that affect the demand for imports and exports

Economic growth
Where there is economic growth, incomes will rise. Some of these incomes will be spent on imports, as demand for imports is 'income-elastic' (demand responds more to a change in income than the change itself).

Inflation
If interest rates are raised by the central bank to control inflation, the currency will look more attractive to foreign investors looking for a high return. Therefore there will be an increase in demand for the currency – and the exchange rate will rise. In addition, the rise in interest rates will encourage saving and reduce spending. The demand for imports will fall.

Economic conditions in other countries
Let's take sterling as an example again. If there is growth in the main countries with which the UK trades, UK exports will tend to increase. This will cause the price of sterling to rise.

The general state of the economy
Suppose the economy is doing well in a particular country. Firms will be encouraged to set up there to be near to their market. This inward investment will raise the exchange rate.

Unemployment
If unemployment is low then demand will increase. This will

further lead to an increase in imports. Equally if there is an increase in demand for UK goods, firms may have to import raw materials in order to manufacture them. Growth in demand for UK goods may therefore mean, in the short term, that the UK has to import more.

The effect of exchange rate movements on a firm

The firm is an exporter

If the exchange rate is rising, it will be more difficult for the firm to export its goods. It may have to accept lower profit margin by dropping the price of its exports, so as to maintain the interest of foreign buyers. In this way the price in terms of a foreign currency may return to the original level. Equally the firm may be re-exporting imported goods, for example raw materials converted to finished goods. It will then benefit from a fall in costs as imports come down in price.

The net effect on the firm depends on whether any fall in exports is compensated for by the seller switching to the domestic economy. If not, the possible effects include:

1. a fall in sales revenue
2. a fall in profits
3. a shortening of the product life cycle
4. having to make workers redundant
5. workers becoming demotivated and insecure, so that productivity drops
6. cash flow suffers as sales fall
7. stocks in the short term rise as goods remain unsold
8. the firm thinks about borrowing

The firm is an importer dealing purely with the domestic market
1. import prices fall
2. the firm may not choose to pass on the price fall and thus increase its profit margin
3. if part of the price fall is passed on then demand rises ...
4. ... recruitment may increase ...

5. ... cash flow increases ...
6. ... and profits rise ...
7. new products may be developed (using the imported material)

This is not a complete list of possible effects. It simply lists the main examples of the impact of exchange rate movements on a firm, to show how the fate of importers and exporters is inextricably linked to currency movements.

The effect of exchange rate movements on the economy

When sterling falls, the prices of imports increase. This may worsen the balance of payments if demand is inelastic (see chapter 6). However, the price of exports will have fallen, so more will be sold causing extra money to come into the economy. This will lead to an increase in demand and a fall in unemployment. But if the economy is already working at full capacity, there is likely to be demand-pull inflation (see chapter 3).

The scenario outlined above could continue as the 'ifs' increase! The key thing to remember is that the effect on the economy must be measured in terms of inflation, unemployment, growth and the balance of payments.

Tutorial: helping you learn

Progress questions
1. What factors affect the demand for exports?

2. If the exchange rate falls, what happens to the price of imports?

3. What is the 'real exchange rate'?

Discussion point
If the UK were to join the European single currency, sterling would have a fixed exchange rate with all of Europe, but a floating one with the rest of the world. If this were to happen, which would

be better – to be an exporter to Europe, or to be an exporter to the rest of the world?

Practical assignment

From the chart below it can be seen that the £ fluctuates against the $ and the DM. Obtain a copy of the accounts of one major exporter and match their profits against the exchange rate movements shown above. Does the trend shown by the £ reflect on the firm's profits?

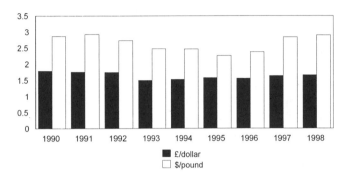

Figure 22. The exchange rate of the pound, the dollar and the DM (deutschmark).

Study/revision tip

If the pound falls, import prices rise and export prices fall. The price of exports goes the same way as the pound, in other words pound up, export prices up.

8

Government Economic Tools

One-minute summary – A government has a variety of economic tools to help it achieve the economic aims of low unemployment, low inflation, economic growth and a balance of payments equilibrium or surplus. These tools can be considered under two main headings: demand side policies and supply side policies. Carrying out such policies will have various effects on firms. In this chapter we will discuss:

▶ supply side policies
▶ demand side policies
▶ effects on a business

Supply side policies

The aim of supply side measures (see chapter 4) is to increase the aggregate supply of resources in the economy. This may take the form of increasing supply of a particular resource or simply making the market work better.

▶ *Example* – If the government subsidises production, the producer will find it more profitable to produce more.

In diagrammatic terms, this may be shown by a shift of the supply curve to the right. Reform of the market – product or labour – will enable the elasticity of supply to increase again and so the price of the product will fall.

Supply side and unemployment
Where vacancies and unemployment co-exist there is a mismatch between aggregate supply and aggregate demand. In other words

labour is occupationally and/or geographically immobile. The government may attempt to:

1. Encourage firms to set up business in areas of high unemployment. This may be done by offering various tax concessions, grants and subsidies.

2. Encourage unemployed people to go elsewhere in search of work. This could be done by transferring benefits and ensuring greater awareness of job vacancies.

3. Improve the occupational mobility of workers. This could be done by ensuring that all unemployed people have access to training courses leading to the supply of skills that are in demand.

4. Reduce the power of trade unions. In this way, wage levels will be less likely to rise above the equilibrium and so unemployed workers will be able to 'price themselves into work'.

Supply side policies and inflation

Inflation may be caused by cost-push or demand-pull pressures. If inflation is caused by a rise in costs, the supply side measures would include:

1. Reduction of the power of trade unions enabling the costs of labour to fall. Under the Thatcher government, for example, trade unions lost their immunity from action against them if workers went on strike. In addition secondary picketing and secondary action were outlawed.

2. Reduction of the power of firms, thereby decreasing monopoly power. This will bring product prices down. Monopoly power was reduced by legislation in 1948 (Monopolies Act), 1965 (Monopolies and Mergers Act), 1973 (Fair Trading Act) and 1980 (Competition Act).

3. Via a policy on incomes, prevent workers from gaining wage

increases in excess of inflation. This is done covertly where governments put 'pay norms' on public sector workers, allowing the whole public sector a pay increase of, for example, 4%. Thus if judges receive 15%, that means there is less available for nurses.

4. Encourage firms to train their workers through investment grants or subsidies. The Labour government introduced measures to 'kick-start' the commercialisation of British science through the University Challenge Fund and the Institute for Enterprise. The Individual Learning Accounts funded an 80% discount on computer literacy courses.

'The New Deal is helping thousands of people it combines a period of personal advice and preparation so participants are ready to start to look for work with quality training, education and work experience options ... all these New Deals aim to equip people claiming benefits so they can compete successfully in the labour market and so secure their economic independence...' (Source: The government's *Annual Report 1998/9*, pages 27/8.)

Supply side policies and economic growth
Supply side policies focus on the potential income in a country. Following such policies may lead to the building of new factories, thereby increasing capacity in the economy. Government may reduce their public expenditure to release funds for the private sector.

Demand side policies

If it is believed that unemployment is caused by too little demand in the economy then, logically, by increasing demand in the economy, unemployment should fall. Equally, if the main cause of inflation is seen as too much demand, then by reducing demand, inflation should fall.

Aggregate demand in the economy is made up of:

1. consumer spending
2. investment expenditure by firms
3. government spending
4. expenditure by foreign residents on a country's goods and services.

In order to increase these variables a government may:

1. Cut income tax, giving employees a rise in disposable income. Demand for normal goods will increase, but may fall for inferior goods.

2. Increase government spending which in turn will increase national income. This will then lead to a rise in demand which will increase employment (demand for labour is derived from demand for the product).

3. Reduce interest rates (unless power to set interest rates has been handed over to the central Bank as in the UK). This will encourage individuals and firms to borrow.

4. Decrease the exchange rate. A depreciation in the exchange rate will cause export costs to fall and import costs to rise.

If demand is stimulated too quickly, then demand will exceed supply. This will lead to demand pull inflation. If this does happen then government and/or the central bank may take anti-inflation measures such as raising interest rates and income tax, and by cutting government expenditure.

The advantage of relying on interest rates as a means of controlling demand is that the rate may be varied far more easily than the rate of income tax. Also, interest rates affect house buyers/ owners primarily and so there is little if any risk of interest involvement.

▶ *Study tip* – Take care when defining particular policies as either supply side or demand side. Some are *both*! For example, a cut in income tax will have demand side effects because disposable income will increase, and thus so will demand. Equally, working will become more attractive to the unemployed since more gross income will be retained. Thus more people will make themselves available for work.

Effects on a business

If the government stimulates demand in the economy, this will lead to an increase in demand for a firm's products (unless the firm is making products that have negative income elasticity, i.e. as incomes rise, demand falls). This may in turn lead to greater recruitment by the firm and (long-term) expansion. Profits and sales revenue will rise and – depending on the firm's ability to increase production – new products will be developed.

If the government encourages supply in the economy, perhaps through greater competition, then firms will become more efficient, or go into liquidation. To become more efficient, costs will be reduced and efforts made to increase workforce productivity.

Tutorial: helping you learn

Progress questions

1. What is meant by a supply side policy?

2. How can a fall in income tax be both a supply-side and a demand-side policy?

3. How will removing worker rights increase the chance of job creation?

4. How will a minimum wage affect employment possibilities?

Discussion point

Supply side measures are long-term measures. Reflation (demand side) is a short-term approach. This short-term approach stores up problems later. What problems are these and how might supply side measures minimise their effects?

Practical assignments

1. Analyse the most recent Budget. Which measures are supply side and which are demand side?

2. Using http://www.hm-treasury.gov.uk/ as a starting point and then going to http://www.labour.org.uk/ on the internet, outline how the Labour government tries to keep inflation and unemployment down and yet at the same time lay the foundations for continued economic growth. If inflation is reduced, will this lead to a rise in unemployment or will the dropping of inflation aid international competitiveness and hence lead to a rise in employment?

3. Starting with the Bank of England's web site at:

   http://www.bankofengland.co.uk/

and then going to:

   http://www.bankofengland.co.uk/geninfo1.htm

prepare arguments for and against the Bank of England having operational responsibility for setting interest rates. In what ways will a rise in interest rates affect an importing, debt-laden manufacturer of fast moving consumer goods?

Study/revision tip
If there is too much demand in the economy then withdrawals may be increased to control it. Withdrawals are savings, tax and imports. Also injections may be reduced. Injections are government spending, investment and exports. The reverse is true for unemployment, in other words injections increase and withdrawals reduce.

9

Published Accounts

One-minute summary – All limited companies have to publish three
main financial statements: the Balance Sheet, the Trading and
Profit and Loss account, and a Cash Statement. It is these
statements that provide the basis for outside analysts to carry out
financial analysis. In this chapter we will discuss:

▶ the Balance Sheet
▶ the Profit and Loss Account
▶ the Cash Flow Statement
▶ the link between the three financial statements

The Balance Sheet

The Balance Sheet is made up of assets, liabilities and capital. An
asset is a resource of the firm. Liabilities are the money owed by the
company to various parties (for example to the government for
tax, directors' loans, and suppliers). Capital represents the owner's
financial interest in the organisation.

We will now look at each category in more detail.

Fixed assets
Fixed assets are resources owned by the firm for the purpose of
aiding the production/selling process. Fixed assets may be tangible
or intangible:

1. Tangible – these are assets with a physical form such as
    premises, machinery, vehicles, plant, fixtures and fittings
    (overheads), and equipment. All of these, with the exception
    of premises, are likely to fall in value. This fall in value is termed
    depreciation.

2. Intangible – These are fixed assets without physical form. Thus a restaurant may have a certain value for its tangible fixed assets but there will be an additional value based on the restaurant's reputation and clientele. This extra invisible value is termed goodwill. Other intangible assets include brand names (such as Heinz), copyright (on this book!), trademarks (for example, Levi).

Current assets

Current assets are short-term assets that change regularly. There are four main categories of current assets:

1. Stock – This covers finished goods, work in progress (part finished goods), raw materials and spares. Stock refers to goods for resale. Therefore it does not include your 'stock' of stationery unless your business is the selling of stationery.

2. Debtors – Debtors arise when goods/services are sold on credit. Debtors may be sold to a third party (debt factoring – the selling of debtors to a third party) to raise cash.

3. Bank – This is the total of all bank balances. If there is an overdraft then 'bank' appears as a liability and goes under 'current liabilities' as 'overdraft'.

4. Cash – Often cash is bracketed with 'bank' as it is unlikely a company will have a large amount of cash in its business for reasons of safety (and lost interest).

Long-term liabilities

These are liabilities where repayment is due in more than one year from the date of the balance sheet. Such items would include bank loans, mortgage or other long-term loans such as a debenture (fixed interest loan).

Current liabilities

These are repayments due within one year from the date of the balance sheet. Current liabilities include:

(a) Overdraft – which is technically repayable on demand

(b) Creditors – the amount owed by the business to suppliers.

Capital

This is an area that often causes problems for students. Capital is the owner's investment in the business. It may be calculated by subtracting total liabilities (current + long term) from total assets (current + fixed). From the subtraction we get a figure for owner's equity or owner's capital. If the business is a company this sum is called 'shareholders funds'. Shareholders' funds thus include:

(a) Shares (preference and ordinary)

(b) Reserves

(c) Retained profit (see next section, this is derived from the Profit and Loss Account).

Profit and Loss Account

The profit and loss account includes three component parts:

1. Trading account

This includes figures detailing the opening stock (stock at the beginning of the trading period), purchases (to include materials for the purpose of making goods for sale) and closing stock (stock at the end of the trading period).

The gross profit is derived from the Trading Account as follows:

Opening stock + purchases – closing stock = cost of goods sold

Sales revenue – cost of goods sold = gross profit

2. Profit and loss Account

This includes indirect expenses incurred during the manufacture and sale of the product. Thus expenses may include administration, interest payable, advertising, rent and rates.

Gross profit – expenses = net profit

3. Appropriation Account

This account shows how the net profit is appropriated (allocated). Some may be paid in tax and dividends. Tax is charged before the payment of dividends. The profit remaining is added to the opening balance (the profit remaining from previous years) and this is the 'retained profit' mentioned in the previous section which appears in the Balance Sheet.

The Cash Flow Statement

Following the 1985 Companies Act, companies now have to publish a Cash Flow Statement in addition to the Balance Sheet and Profit & Loss account. This statement uses information from the accounting records and shows an overall view of money flowing in and out of a business during an accounting period. It is *not* a forecast but an historic document. In other words, it shows what has happened (rather than what it is expected will happen).

The links between the three financial statements

1. The Profit and Loss Account focuses on the profitability of the business. The Balance Sheet focuses on the asset strength of the business. The Cash Flow Statement shows the liquidity of the business. (Note however, as shown in chapter 13, liquidity ratios may be calculated from the Balance Sheet).

2. Sales are made for both cash and credit. When the money is received it appears as a cash inflow in the Cash Flow Statement; while waiting for the receipt, the customers are debtors and so would appear in any Balance Sheet. There is no distinction in the Trading Account between sales for cash and sales on credit.

3. If a business buys a fixed asset, money goes out of the bank account and is shown as a cash outflow on the Cash Flow Statement. The fixed asset will appear in the Balance Sheet.

4. A productivity bonus paid to workers would be a cash outflow

and would also diminish the bank balance. Wages appear in the Profit and Loss Account.

5. Capital is injected into the business. This appears as capital in the Balance Sheet and also as a cash inflow in the Cash Flow Statement.

Tutorial: helping you learn

Progress questions
1. What is 'capital'?
2. What items are shown on a Balance Sheet?
3. How are gross profit and net profit calculated?

Discussion point
What information – in addition to that shown in the published documents – would a financial analyst need to know about a company before giving advice to a prospective investor?

Practical assignments
1. Obtain a copy of any public limited company's accounts. Make a list of the various terms included in the published accounts that are not covered in this chapter. Typically these would include ACT (Advance Corporation Tax) and Minority interest.

2. Carefully distinguish between 'shareholders' capital', 'owner's equity', and 'capital employed'.

3. Show how:

   (a) a loan from the bank and
   (b) a reduction in the price of a product

   will lead to entries in the various financial statements.

4. It has been suggested that Marks and Spencers is likely to be

taken over. In 1999 they were heavily criticised for their lack-lustre profits performance. By going to the web site:

http://www.marks-and-spencer.co.uk/default.asp

comment on the image of Marks and Spencers. Go to www.ft.com and order a set of Marks and Spencers published accounts and calculate ten key ratios from the accounts. In terms of image of the company and their financial strengths and weaknesses, what makes M&S attractive to a possible take over? Tesco (http://www.tesco.co.uk/indexn.htm) are rumoured to be one of the companies interested in a takeover what advantages does M&S offer to Tesco?

Study/revision tips
1. The Balance Sheet is a financial statement shown at the end of the trading year. It is a snapshot of the financial standing of a business.

$$\text{Assets} = \text{Capital} + \text{Liabilities}$$

2. The Trading & Profit and Loss Account summarises the revenue and expenses of a business for a set accounting period and shows the overall profit and loss.

$$\text{Revenue minus expenses} = \text{profit or loss}$$

3. The Cash Flow Statement uses information from the accounting records, and shows an historic overall view of money flowing in and out of the business.

10

Sources of Finance

One-minute summary – Every business needs finance to start up. It will also need finance to keep the business going – in particular until it receives its first revenue. Finance will be necessary for assets such as buildings, fixtures and fittings. The business will also need finance for stock and wages. The former is asset finance; the latter is working capital finance. In this chapter we will discuss:

▶ definition and classification of finance
▶ short-term sources of finance
▶ medium-term sources of finance
▶ long-term sources of finance
▶ other sources of finance

Definition and classification of finance

Asset finance
A business needs finance to cover the cost of essential assets. Examples of these essential assets are:

1. equipment
2. transport
3. shop fittings
4. premises

The business organisation must have some or all of these before it can start business activity. To buy, rent or lease these items, they will need asset finance.

Working capital finance
The business also needs finance to pay for day to day running costs.

These will include the purchase of materials, paying wages and being able to offer credit to customers.

Classification
Finance may be classified by:

(a) duration, whether it is short-term, mid-term or long-term finance.

(b) whether it is internal (sourced by profits, sale of assets) or external (sourced by trade credit, bank overdrafts, or factoring).

(c) whether it takes the form of debt (loan) or equity (issue of shares).

Short-term sources of finance (0–3 years)

This is essentially working capital finance. Typical sources are:

Bank overdraft
This is a high cost form of finance but interest is only charged on the actual amount borrowed. The loan is unsecured and in theory the bank can demand repayment of the overdraft at any time.

Trade credit
This finance is provided by suppliers; the business buys goods and materials on credit. The longer the payment is delayed, the more the debtor gains but there is always a risk that in future the supplier will demand payment in advance.

Debt factoring
If a business is suffering from late payment by debtors, it may sell these debts to a third party. Thus if a business is owed £30,000 by a debtor, it can sell that debt to a third party (a factor) for say £28,000. The factor gains £2,000 profit, but also takes on the risk and the administration costs of chasing a potentially errant debtor.

Medium term finance (3–10 years)

This finance is used to purchase fixed assets as well as to provide working capital finance, thus it is used for both asset and working capital finance.

Hire purchase agreement

This method of finance is simply deferring total payment of assets. A deposit is put down at the beginning of the agreement and assets are then paid for by instalment. Although the total is greater than the original figure, breathing space is acquired as payments are staggered over a period of months or years.

Lease purchase

This is similar to hire purchase but no deposit is payable. Ownership does not pass, therefore the lessee is paying for the use of the asset. This 'use' will include maintenance provided by the lessor. Tax relief is claimable against lease payments.

Sale and leaseback

The business sells a fixed asset such as a building. It then leases the building back. The short-term cost of the lease is far less than the money received for the sale. Thus the business has generated cash, but in the long run will incur higher outgoings. In addition the business will no longer own the asset and so will not be able to sell it or use it for collateral in the future.

Long-term finance (10+ years)

Long term finance is either debt or equity. Debt finance is raised through loans either via mortgages or the issue of debentures. A debenture is a fixed rate interest loan and redeemable after a fixed period. Mortgages are used to purchase property. Interest is charged at a fixed or variable rate.

Equity finance involves the sale of shares in a business. A share owner is entitled to vote at the Annual General Meeting and also to receive any dividends paid. Shares have no maturity date and therefore cannot be repaid. The more shares are issued to outside parties, the greater control is diluted.

Other forms of capital

Venture capital

Venture capital is high risk capital. In the UK there are more than a hundred venture capital funds. The money is offered by:

1. pension funds
2. insurance companies
3. banks
4. investment trusts
5. industrial corporations
6. regional development agencies
7. private individuals.

Venture capitalists are looking for:

(a) A product pitched at a big market.

(b) A product that the investors are actually interested in. Some funds, for example, invest in early stage capital but others don't. So, even if your idea is a good one, it won't matter much if you try to get late stage specialists to look at your proposal. Usually, they won't.

(c) Evidence of a good track record in management.

(d) A quick return on the money invested for example within three to four years.

(e) Evidence of a clear business plan with targets against which performance can be measured.

(f) A company that has identified its weaknesses and has a strategy to deal with them.

(g) A clear understanding of the competitors and their strengths and weaknesses.

Government finance

Government finance is available on a European, national or local basis.

European finance may be available from the European Investment Bank. Under article 130 of the Treaty of Rome the European Investment Bank is empowered to ensure 'the balanced and steady development of the community by means of providing loans or loan guarantees to member states for projects which will enable individual member states to work towards EU goals ...'

National government help is available through the Loan Guarantee Scheme and a variety of grants if the business is in a certain area, such as Assisted Areas or regions falling within the scope of the various Single Regeneration Budget programmes.

The Loan Guarantee Scheme is designed to help new and established small businesses with an annual turnover of no more than £1.5 million. The Department of Trade and Industry provides security by guaranteeing 70% of the loan (or 85% if you have been trading for more than 2 years). In return, the business pays a premium to the DTI of 1.5% a year of the outstanding loan.

Other grants available include the SMART grant which provides up to 75% of the cost of feasibility and technical studies and up to 30% of development costs.

Local authorities

Local authorities provide help in terms of grants, premises, advice and loans. Details are available from the local Business Link and/or Training and Enterprise Centre. (TEC).

Youth schemes

Some schemes such as the Prince's Youth Business Trust and Livewire are aimed at young people in particular.

Tutorial: helping you learn

Progress questions

1. List three sources of external finance.

2. What is a debenture?

3. What is equity capital?
4. What are the disadvantages of raising finance by issuing shares?

Discussion point
What are the main factors affecting the source of finance? Which ones are most important and why?

Practical assignments
1. Visit your local Business Link office and assess the various local sources of finance available. Prepare a business plan to submit to a venture capital fund in the hope of raising capital. What information will you require from them before accepting any help offered?

2. One way of raising finance is through merger. By accessing:

    http://news2.thls.bbc.co.uk/hi/english/business/news-
    id%5F562000/562640.stm

    outline the timetable to a merger. Explain why the DTI have given up merger powers.

    http://news2.thls.bbc.co.uk/hi/english/business/
    the_economy/newsid_413000/413640.stm

3. When individuals wish to buy a house they often have to raise a mortgage. Problems are caused not by there being too few companies to choose from but by there being too many options. It is now possible to compare mortgages online so in theory the price of mortgages should come down:

    http://news2.thls.bbc.co.uk/hi/english/business/news-
    id%5F615000/615556.stm

    In what ways are the methods available to raise finance for a company and an individual, similar? By accessing the following web site, outline the key questions one should ask before taking out a mortgage.

    http://news2.thls.bbc.co.uk/hi/english/business/news-
    id%5F607000/607323.stm

Study/revision point
The most common source of finance for a business already trading is retained profit. No interest is chargeable and control is not diluted.

11

Break-Even Analysis

One-minute summary – Break-even is a level of output at which there is neither profit nor loss. If a firm manages to sell more than the break-even point then a profit will be made. Break-even may be measured in terms of volume or revenue. The break-even graph may be used to show break-even, margin of safety, changes in price and a change in investment and its impact on break-even. In this chapter we will discuss:

▶ a definition of break-even
▶ key components of a break-even analysis
▶ key formulae
▶ plotting a break-even graph
▶ using a break-even graph
▶ criticisms of break-even analysis

A definition of break-even

A break-even level of output is where there is no profit or loss. If we wish to illustrate this graphically, then break-even will be where total cost equals total revenue. The break-even chart is shown overleaf and we see that where total revenue equals total costs (fixed costs plus variable costs) then we have break-even.

Key components of a break-even analysis
Several key definitions have to be learned before you can carry out a break-even analysis.

Variable costs
These are costs that vary directly in line with production. For example, if production doubles then so do variable costs. Typically these would be the costs of direct labour and direct materials.

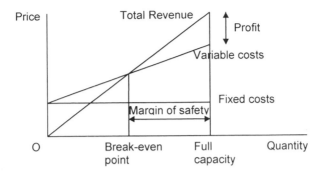

Figure 23. A break-even analysis graph.

Semi-variable costs

These are costs that vary but not because of changes in production. Thus a telephone account is a semi-variable cost. Its cost varies, but not in line with production.

Fixed costs

These are costs that do not vary at all. Good examples are rent and rates. Costs like these stay the same irrespective of day to day output.

Margin of safety

This is the difference between the current level of output and the break-even point. In the graph illustrating the definition, we can see that the margin of safety is shown in terms of units. This shows how much production can fall without the business turning a profit into a loss.

Sales revenue

This means the total revenue from sales. It is found by multiplying price by volume of output.

Total costs

This is calculated by adding together total variable cost and total fixed costs.

Unit contribution

This is the contribution made towards fixed costs and profit by the sale of one unit. It is found by subtracting the variable cost per unit from the selling price. Thus:

unit contribution = selling price less variable costs per unit

Key formulae

Break-even point

$$\frac{\text{Fixed costs}}{\text{Unit contribution}}$$

Total contribution

Unit contribution multiplied by volume of output.

Profit

Total contribution less fixed costs.

Break-even point (in sales revenue)

$$\frac{\text{Fixed costs}}{\text{Contribution per unit}} \text{ x price per unit}$$

Margin of safety

Current output less break-even point.

Profit

Margin of safety multiplied by contribution per unit.

Target profit

$$\frac{\text{Desired net income}}{1 - \text{tax rate}}$$

Level of sales required to achieve target profit (in units)

$$\frac{\text{fixed costs} + \text{target profit}}{\text{contribution per unit}}$$

Plotting a break-even graph

Too often, students start plotting the break-even graph without doing the calculations first. After ten minutes, they find that their scale is too big and they have to start again, wasting precious examination time. For all break-even questions the following rules should be followed:

1. Calculate the total sales revenue.

2. Calculate the break-even point (which will act as a check against the accuracy of your graph).

3. Plot the axes (total sales revenue will be the highest line).

4. Draw the fixed costs. These should be represented by a straight line drawn horizontally across the graph.

5. Draw in the sales revenue.

6. Calculate the total costs (total variable costs + total fixed costs).

7. Draw in the total costs.

8. Make sure the graphical representation of break-even matches your calculations.

9. Make sure you label all the lines and, if asked, that you can show where profit, break-even, loss and margin of safety are.

Using a break-even graph

The break-even graph can be used to illustrate the results of different decisions.

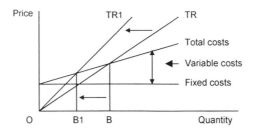

Figure 24. The impact on profits of a change in price.

The above graph shows the impact on profits of a change in price. Notice how TR1 means that break-even is earlier and thus the price must have risen. This shows that if the price is raised, then break-even is at B1. Market research can try and establish whether if the price rose, consumer demand would be sufficient to reach the break-even point. This version of the graph may thus be linked to your study of pricing policy.

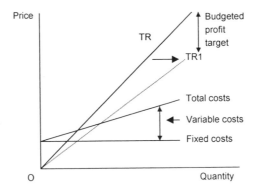

Figure 25. A break-even chart for decision-making.

The above graph shows how the break-even graph may be used in a discussion on profit targets.

Worked example
Selling price = £6
Variable costs = £4

Fixed costs = £200,000
Target profit = £500,000

From the above, we know that break-even is calculated thus:

$$\text{Break-even} = \frac{\text{fixed costs}}{\text{unit contribution}}$$

$$\text{Therefore} \quad \frac{£200,000}{£6 - £4} = \frac{£200,000}{£2} = 100,000 \text{ units}$$

Since the target profit is £500,000, we adjust the formula:

$$\text{Level of output needed} = \frac{\text{fixed costs} + \text{target profit}}{\text{unit contribution}}$$

$$\text{Therefore} \quad \frac{£700,000}{£6 - £4} = \frac{£700,000}{£2} = 350,000 \text{ units}$$

If the price is lowered then the contribution is lowered and so more have to be sold to reach the target profits. The diagram above shows this.

The break-even chart can also be adapted to show the impact of new investment.

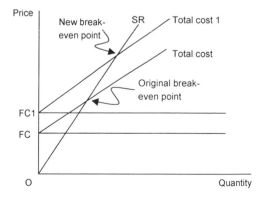

Figure 26. A break-even chart showing the impact
of a rise in fixed costs.

In the diagram above we see that a rise in fixed costs means that we have to sell more to break-even.

We can also use this diagram when considering investment as the decision whether the company can afford to buy will depend on whether market research shows the new break-even point can be reached. In other words, can the volume of sales be increased?

Criticisms of break-even analysis

The main criticisms of this technique lie in the assumptions that have to be made. For example:

1. Costs cannot easily be divided up into fixed or variable. Semi-variable costs are not included in the formula.

2. It is assumed that all sales are at the same price. If discounts are available for bulk purchases, then the sales revenue line will not be linear.

3. Possible economies of scale are ignored. If such economies were to be incorporated, the total cost line would curve.

4. The break-even chart ignores external events such as the state of the economy that would affect prices and costs.

5. Fixed costs would change at different levels of activity, for example with the purchase of machinery.

Tutorial: helping you learn

Progress questions
1. What is the formula for break-even?

2. What does 'contribution' mean?

3. How is sales revenue calculated?

4. Where does the total cost line start from?

Discussion point
Given all the criticisms of the break-even chart, what is the point of drawing one? If any decision is based on a simple break-even chart (which ignores any changes in variable costs per unit and selling price) is it not more likely that an incorrect decision will be made?

Practical assignment
Try to find out the costs associated with your tuition in Business Studies. This will include for example the teacher's salary (pro rata) and the costs of heating and lighting. If each pupil paid £5 an hour, how many would it take for the institution to break-even? Draw a graph to illustrate the profit.

If you are attending a fee-paying establishment, draw and plot the estimated profit made from your enrolment at the school. Clearly state your assumptions and include fixed costs such as prospectuses and advertising in your calculations.

Study/revision tip
Always do your calculations before drawing the graph.

12

Inward Investment

One-minute summary – 'Inward investment' means investment in a
country by firms from overseas. The government encourages
inward investment because it provides jobs and an injection of
capital. That said, the presence of firms from overseas is sometimes
blamed for unemployment here. The UK is an attraction for
overseas investors – and yet if the main attraction is that Britain is a
'gateway to Europe' investors could have gone to other European
countries. Clearly there must be other factors affecting inward
investment. In this chapter we will discuss:

▶ types of investment
▶ inward investment to the UK – the figures
▶ what makes the UK so attractive
▶ legislation for inward investors to be aware of

Types of investment

'Inward investment' refers to investment into a country from
firms/countries elsewhere/in other countries. Thus if Honda were
to build a plant in Swindon, that would be inward investment
(from Britain's point of view) but outward investment from the
point of view of Japan. Investment may be categorised as tangible
and intangible.

Tangible
1. plant
2. machinery
3. buildings.

Intangible
1. research and development

2. technology acquisition
3. design
4. human resources
5. information structures
6. the ways in which work is organised
7. labour relations
8. management structures
9. the formation of technological and commercial links with other firms and with suppliers and customers
10. market exploration and development, advertising and after-sales service
11. in-house development and acquisition of bespoke software.

Inward investment to the UK – the figures

▶ *The 1999 results* – 'In the year ended March 1999, IBB (Investment in Britain Bureau) recorded a total of 652 new investments (204 new projects, 250 expansions by companies already based in the UK, and 198 major acquisitions). These projects created 44,413 new jobs and safeguarded another 74,340. At the end of 1998, stock of inward investments into the UK were £196.4bn, an increase of 30 per cent on the previous year amounting to 8% of the total world-wide stock of foreign direct investment.' (Source: Office for National Statistics.)

What makes the UK so attractive?

The UK provides the right economic conditions
1. The UK is the second most successful developed country for attracting foreign investment. There are 4,200 American companies, 1,600 German ones, 1,300 from France and 1,000 from Japan already here.

2. Relatively low taxation.

3. Skilled and motivated English-speaking workforce.

4. Convenient access to Europe.

5. London is a leading international financial centre.

6. Industrial relations – the UK strike rate has been below the EU average each year since 1986.

7. Within the EU the UK has 25% of all inward investment, and over 40% of Japanese investment.

8. Tax encouragements to businesses include the cut in corporation tax from 33% to 31% from 1 April 1997 and from 31% to 30% with effect from 1 April 1999.

9. Britain has the eighth biggest economy in the world.

Incentives to invest

1. Regional Selective Assistance – this is available for projects in parts of the UK needing investment to revitalise their economies.

2. Project Grant is the main type of assistance. It is based on a project's capital expenditure costs and the number of jobs it is expected to create or safeguard, normally in its first three years. A grant is negotiated according to the amount considered necessary to enable the project to go ahead in the form proposed.

3. Local Authority Assistance: local authorities in England and Wales have a specific power under Part III of the Local Government and Housing Act 1989 to promote the economic development of their area.

The Single Regeneration Budget

The Single Regeneration Budget provides flexible support for sustainable regeneration, economic development and industrial competitiveness in England in a way that meets specific local needs and priorities. The money is distributed via the European Investment Bank.

A skilled labour force

The UK workforce is especially skilled in those sectors where foreign direct investment is most extensive - electronics, engineering, science, information technology, telecommunications and finance, among others.

Wage levels

Britain has low labour costs relative to other industrialised countries because of low social on-costs. These include financing a voluntary sick pay or pension scheme and participation in state schemes.

Availability of property facilities

The UK has government, industrial and commercial premises available for sale or rent in the Assisted Areas of the country, some of them new, others previously occupied. Newer factories generally range from very small workshops of 50 square metres (about 500 square feet) up to 2,300 square metres (about 23,000 square feet). Larger premises may be available on some estates.

Taxation

The main corporation tax rate is currently 31% and the rate for many small companies is lower still - just 21%. The downward trend in taxation, which started in the early 1980s with the Thatcher government, increases the attraction of the UK when compared to other countries. Low corporation tax releases funds for investment; low income tax acts as an encouragement for people to find work.

Supply sources

The Regional Supply Network has extensive knowledge of supply companies nationwide, assisting both purchasers and suppliers alike, and offers professional advice on procurement. There are ten Regional Supply Offices (RSOs), each operated by a partnership of Regional Development Organisations, Business Links, Training & Enterprise Councils and other business support organisations.

Global communications
Britain has the most liberalised and competitive telecommunications market in Europe. Successive UK governments have ensured that competition is promoted in telecommunications.

Using the UK as an export base
As a member of the European Union, the UK is also part of the world's largest fully developed trading market.

Legislation for inward investors to be aware of

Inward investors must be aware of the following legislation, not only because they will have to comply, but also certain items – such as the Minimum Wages Act – will affect the firm's variable costs, and may also act as a deterrent to come to Britain.

National Minimum Wage
This took effect from April 1999.

The European Working Time Directive
Applicable since 1 October 1998, this legislation has created an entitlement for employees to minimum daily and weekly rest periods, a limit of 48 hours on the average time which employees can be required to work in a week, and restrictions on night work. Certain exclusions apply.

European Social Policy
The Government views the Social Agreement as an opportunity to introduce fair minimum standards of treatment at work to which all employees are entitled. Four directives have so far been adopted under the agreement:

1. The European Works Council Directive requires companies with at least 1,000 EU employees and at least 150 workers in each of two member states, to establish structures for consulting workers on issues that affect them.

2. The Parental Leave Directive gives parents at work the right to up to three months' unpaid leave on the birth or adoption of a child, and the right for employees to time off for urgent family reasons.

3. The Part-Time Workers Directive entitles part-time workers to the same employment rights as full-time workers.

4. The Burden of Proof in Sex Discrimination Directive will, once a prima facie case has been made, place the onus on the defendant (usually the employer) to prove that sex discrimination has not occurred. The UK has until July 2001 to implement this directive.

Environmental legislation
1. Environmental Protection Act 1990
2. Environment Act 1995
3. Town and Country Planning Act 1990
4. Town and Country Planning (Assessment of Environmental Effects) Regulations 1988
5. Planning (Hazardous Substances) Act 1990
6. Control of Pollution (Special Regulations) 1980
7. Health and Safety at Work Act 1974
8. Management of Health and Safety at Work Regulations 1992
9. Water Resources Act 1991
10. Water Industry Act 1991.

Tutorial: helping you learn

Progress questions
1. State three pieces of legislation which concern environmental protection.

2. What are the main reasons why the UK is attractive as a place for investment?

Discussion point

The UK has 1% of the world's population and yet gets 8% of the world's cross-border direct investment. In 1998 the United Nations Conference on Trade and Development estimated that Britain's stock of foreign direct investment was $274bn – nearly double the German figure.

Practical assignments

1. Go to the Invest in Britain Bureau web site and assess the UK performance for inward investment:

    http://www.dti.gov.uk/IBB/flash/index.html

2. Does the UK current economic performance encourage or discourage inward investors?

3. Will the UK's non-joining of the single currency discourage inward investment?

4. 'Britain has consolidated its place as the number one destination for inward investment in Europe, despite being outside the Euro, according to US management consultants at Kearney. Furthermore, only 3% of directors at the world's largest companies say they will cut investment to those countries, like Britain and Switzerland, who remain outside the Euro.' Source: *Daily Telegraph, 1 July 1999.*

    (a) Outline the main factors a multinational considers before investing in one particular country.

    (b) What makes the UK such an attractive place in which to invest?

    (c) What is the role of the DTI in encouraging inward investment? (See: http://www.dti.gov.uk/).

Study/revision tip

Investment in the UK will create jobs. The main attraction to the UK of overseas investment is, quite simply, the UK wants them and so the government offers a variety of incentives to encourage firms to invest.

13

Financial Ratios

One-minute summary – Financial ratios are the main method used to compare companies' performance. There are non-financial ratios (see chapter 17) but business studies syllabuses tend to concentrate on the financial ones. Ratios may be grouped under several different headings, such as 'liquidity'. Usually examinations put the emphasis on interpretation rather than number-crunching. In this chapter we will discuss:

▶ profitability ratios
▶ liquidity ratios
▶ efficiency ratios
▶ investment gearing and shareholders' ratios
▶ the limitation of ratio analysis

Profitability ratios

These are ratios that measure the profitability of the business. This involves a comparison of profits with either the cost of sales or sales revenue.

Gross profit margin

$$\frac{\text{Gross profit}}{\text{Sales revenue}} \times 100$$

This shows the percentage of gross profit that is available to pay for overheads. Note that overheads and other expenses may increase in a bid to boost sales, for example through advertising. This will not be shown by the gross profit mark-up. This is one reason why other ratios such as 'administration:sales' are used.

Gross profit mark-up

$$\frac{\text{Gross profit}}{\text{Cost of sales}} \times 100$$

Mark-up is the amount of profit that is added to the cost of goods sold. For example, if the cost of goods sold = £5 and the mark-up is 20%, the sales price will be £6. If the market is elastic, it is likely the price will be low. In this case, we would expect sales to increase (in both volume and value) but there will be a low mark-up.

Price is affected by a wide variety of factors, such as stock, image, competition, the economic environment, and legislation. Also, it is unwise to consider only one interpretation of a low mark-up.

Net profit margin

$$\frac{\text{Net profit}}{\text{Sales revenue}} \times 100$$

This ratio shows the operational efficiency of a business. No reference is made to the method by which the business is financed (shares or borrowed funds). This ratio is more reliable than gross profit because it takes into account expenses. In the same way, the acid test ratio is more reliable than the current ratio described in the next section because it takes into account stock.

Liquidity ratios

Also known as the acid test ratio, the formula is:

$$\frac{\text{Current assets} - \text{stock}}{\text{Current liabilities}}$$

There is another test of liquidity known as the 'current ratio'. This is current assets divided by current assets. However, the acid test ratio is a better test of liquidity, since stock is the least liquid of the current assets (current assets = stock, debtors, bank and cash).

Stock may be included in a ratio designed to show a firm's ability to repay current liabilities, but this it is likely to convey the wrong impression. Thus if the current ratio is 4:1, the investor may think that the business is solvent. However, if 3.5 of the 4 consists of stock, the business is in a far worse state and far less solvent – than was first imagined.

Efficiency ratios

Trade debtor collection period

$$\frac{\text{Average trade debtors} \times 365}{\text{Total credit sales}}$$

This shows the length of time it is before deals made on credit are satisfied. The longer the period, the worse the cash flow. Extension of credit may lead to more sales. These extra debtors may then be sold to a factor who, by persistent reminders to pay, may actually alienate them from the original seller.

Stock turnover

$$\frac{\text{Cost of goods sold}}{\text{Average stockholding}}$$

The stock turnover ratio measures the efficiency of stock management. Care must be taken to recognise that the 'stock' figure is the average stock. This is found by taking opening + closing stock and then dividing the answer by two. The ratio indicates how many months/days cash is tied up. Thus a stock turnover of 3 indicates that we have, on average, 4 months' stock.

High stock is not necessarily a bad sign (new product, expected increases in demand, vertical integration). Again it must be stressed that ratios are just figures. We need to know the reasons behind the calculations – some of which may be found in the Chairman's Report which companies append to their annual accounts.

Investment gearing and shareholders' ratios

Gearing

$$\frac{\text{borrowed funds (to include preference shares)}}{\text{equity}}$$

This ratio measures a firm's capital structure. It shows the relationship between long-term liabilities (borrowed funds) and the total capital employed (share capital, reserves and long term loans).

This ratio differs in various textbooks. For example, some textbooks include a firm's overdraft as a liability – despite the fact that it is not long-term. A point worth stressing is that it is more important to be consistent when conducting ratio analysis than it is to be accurate (although, obviously, both accuracy and consistency are desirable).

If a company is highly geared and profits are high, the shareholders should gain as despite the high pay out in interest, there will not be many shareholders (in comparison with low gearing) to share the remainder. Equally if the business is low-geared and the company makes low profits then interest payments will be low (in total) leaving funds for shareholders, albeit shared among a greater number.

Firms that are highly geared with low profits may find themselves being wound up (either compulsorily or voluntarily) as they will be unable to keep up with interest payments. If the Bank of England raises interest rates in pursuit of an anti-inflation policy, a highly geared firm one which raises most of its capital through debt – will suffer in having to pay higher interest payments. The high interest rates will also cause demand to fall, reducing the company's profits.

Price earnings ratio

$$\frac{\text{Market price per share}}{\text{Earnings per share}}$$

For many investors the 'P/E' ratio is the main one to consider when they looking at companies with a view to purchasing shares.

The market price shows the confidence of the market in your business, *but* this confidence may be misplaced. Perhaps strident speeches at the firm's AGM (Annual General Meeting) stressing the profitability in the forthcoming year will not be believed if in previous years the firm has not kept to its projections. The higher the P/E ratio, the more confident the market is that the earnings per share will either be maintained or improved.

Problems with ratios

1. It is difficult to compare like with like, for example to find two companies producing exactly the same type of products and with the same accounting periods.

2. Accounting records are often a year old. Thus the snapshot given by ratio analysis may no longer be true today.

3. The figures for the accounts may have been 'massaged'. Stock, for example, could be work-in-progress and this figure is based on estimates. Equally the depreciation percentage may have been changed, or the bad debt provision increased.

4. The figures do not show the reasons behind the decisions that lead to these results. Is holding high stocks a deliberate plan, or was it a result of unexpectedly low demand? Did profits rise because of the efficiency of this business, or because exchange rates rose and this business happens to deal with the domestic market?

5. Other data is needed such as labour turnover, competitors' strategy, the economic environment – interest rates, taxes and economic growth as these will affect demand.

Tutorial: helping you learn

Progress questions

1. Write the formula for, and explain, the gearing ratio.

2. Write the formula for, and explain, the debtors' collection period ratio.

3. What are the disadvantages of relying solely on ratios to tell you about a company's performance?

Discussion points

1. 'Inter-firm comparison' happens where similar firms

anonymously submit key financial data. In return, they receive competitors' data to allow them to make comparisons. Give examples of incorrect interpretations based on sets of figures.

2. Critics of ratio analysis point to several weaknesses such as the reasons behind the figures are not shown and differences in accounting policies among firms. Given such criticisms (and others), is it likely that some other form of appraisal will one day replace ratio analysis?

Practical assignments

1. Using the *Financial Times* (or go to: http://www.ft.com on the internet) order a set of accounts for a football club such as Tottenham Hotspur. Assess the proportion of revenue that comes from merchandising, television fees, transfer fees, and attendances. What does this analysis tell you about the football club?

2. By going to http://www.marks-and-spencer.co.uk/default.asp and also http://www.tesco.co.uk/indexn.htm assess and compare the two companies without using ratio analysis. When this is finished, only then compare ratios. Make recommendations to a third party about the viability of a take over bid. Extract five key ratios; focus on them and explain which company is likely to take over the other.

Revision/study tip

A ratio is only as good as the accuracy of the figures which are used. However, if you do have to do calculations in your examinations, show your workings. Even if you arrive at the wrong answer, you will still receive credit for arriving at the wrong answer in the right manner!

14

Advertising

One-minute summary – When advertising a product there is a wide choice of media available. With the growth of the internet, a new option is offered. Web design is not the same as designing an advertisement for television, radio or posters. The pages may be interactive and involve video clips – and the identity of the observer may be recorded. Despite this new option the criteria for choosing media is still the same. The role of the Advertising Standards Authority has also remained unchanged but its scope has widened to incorporate (as far as possible) advertising via the net. In this chapter we will discuss:

▶ choice of media
▶ evaluation of media
▶ the role of the Advertising Standards Authority

Choice of media

When choosing the appropriate media the following key factors should be considered:

The type of product being offered

Some products are more suited to certain types of media. Those that need to be seen in action to be effective are likely to use a medium that combines sound, vision, colour and movement.

Some products are restricted in their choice of advertising; cigarette advertising was banned on television long before a ban was even considered for newspapers.

The target audience

The audience can be closely identified when using television as a medium. The companies involved have a breakdown of their audience – though the advent of the remote control button and teletext means that the showing of an advertisement is just as likely to be the time that other channels/teletext are accessed.

Exclusiveness of the media
If the media is very selective as with a subscription-only magazine – then the advertisement can be targeted at exactly the right group. In addition, the magazine owners are likely to have detailed information about their subscribers such as their age, interests, gender, name and address.

Costs
Cost can be considered as a total cost, or a cost per thousand readers/viewers, or costs as a percentage of expected return. Plainly it would be a waste for an individual restaurateur to advertise on national television, since the restaurant's likely clientele would live within a comparatively short distance, whereas a restaurant chain with regional/national outlets throughout the broadcast area may well find it cost effective.

Impact of the media
Radio allows jingles to support the advertisement but will the message (rather than the music) be remembered? Posters may be good for initial impact but passers-by often have only a few seconds to read any words.

Shelf-life of the advertisement
If the advertisement is in a magazine then, potentially, it may be active for a number of years as old magazines typically languish in dentists' surgeries and other public areas.

A web site can last indefinitely provided it is updated on a regular basis.

Evaluation of the media

Newspapers and magazines
Advantages
(a) targeted audience
(b) low cost per potential reader
(c) use of colour
(d) local flavour (if using local newspapers)
(e) can include a tear-off segment.

Disadvantages
(a) no sound or movement
(b) placement may be in the hands of the publisher
(c) may be passed over by the reader.

Television
Advantages
(a) Combines sound, vision, colour and movement.
(b) Facilitates phone-in ordering.
(c) A theme may be built up (as in the Oxo advertisements).
(d) High national and local coverage.
(e) Details on the likely audience is available.
(f) Advertising may be linked to a television programme.
(g) A particular time may be booked, such half-time in the Rugby World Cup Final.

Disadvantages
(a) There are high initial costs.
(b) The remote control button means the advertisement may not be seen.
(c) Video machines are now available that exclude the advertisement from any recording.
(d) Time means the impact has to be immediate.

Cinema
Advantages
(a) Advertisements may have a very local flavour ('Eat at The Taj Mahal Restaurant within 5 minutes of this cinema').

(b) There is a low cost per member of the audience.

(c) There is a captive audience and *no* remote control button!

Disadvantages

(a) Cinema is unlikely to offer a phone-in facility.

(b) Many distractions the advertising interval is the main time that people arrive, chat, buy refreshments etc.

Radio

Advantages

(a) Low cost

(b) Can ally music with the message

(c) Local radio means that advertisements may be targeted

Disadvantages

(a) Audience may be only half-listening (car radio)

(b) Unlikely to be able to allow any follow-up

Internet

Advantages

(a) Web sites are easy to update.

(b) Low cost maintenance.

(c) Low cost to set up.

(d) Visitors may be 'trapped' by special coding making it difficult for them to move off the site – though this technique should be used with caution as it may annoy people and deter future visits.

(e) Some customer knowledge is available such as their IP number and type of browser.

(f) Direct customer input is available via feedback forms.

(g) The use of colour, sound and movement is available to add interest.

Disadvantages

(a) Many visitors may distrust online financial transactions.

(b) There are new opportunities for fraud.

(c) The internet is difficult to police

(d) Accuracy of commercial information is hard to check

The role of the Advertising Standards Authority

The purpose of the Advertising Standards Authority is to ensure that all advertisements wherever they are placed are:

(a) legal
(b) decent
(c) honest
(d) truthful

The Codes of advertising practice were updated in 1995 to include non-broadcast electronic media. This means that, as well as all other non-broadcast advertisements, the Codes now cover those on CD-rom, computer and video games.

▶ *Note* – Under the Codes, the normal judicial burden of proof is reversed; advertisers must prove to the ASA that their claims are true. The ASA does not enforce the law but refers complaints which fall directly under legislation to the appropriate law enforcement body.

The Authority will:

1. investigate complaints about UK advertisements
2. undertake research
3. give advice to help advertisers to follow the Codes.

According to Matti Alderson, the ASA Director General:

'Statutory control of the internet is virtually impossible, but the net lends itself well to a system of self-regulation and consumers can have confidence in the advertising they respond to on the site if it is seen to be legal, decent, honest and truthful. It is through using the industry's Codes that the net can flourish as a credible advertising medium.'

The ASA and the law
In 1978 the Office of Fair Trading investigated the ASA and self-

regulation. In 1980 the Department of Trade and Industry also reviewed the ASA. The Government decided, in light of these reviews, that the system was working well but that some further legislation could provide a better framework for the ASA to operate in.

Legislation was introduced in 1984 through an EC Directive on Misleading Advertising. The Directive was implemented in the UK as the Control of Misleading Advertisements Regulations 1988. The ASA was officially recognised as an 'established means' for controlling the content of non-broadcast advertisements. This provided the Authority with an additional sanction to refer persistent or deliberate offenders to the Office of Fair Trading for action through the courts.

Tutorial: helping you learn

Progress questions
1. 'Every advertisement must be legal, ...' Complete the sentence.

2. State two advantages of advertising on the radio.

3. What products are best advertised on the internet?

Discussion point
How can advertising on the internet be policed?

Practical assignment
The tenth Code of Advertising Practice was issued on the 1st October 1999. How does this code differ from the previous codes?

Study/revision tips
An advertisement that is designed without the product and the audience in mind will fail – however sophisticated the media!

15

Pricing

One-minute summary – When pricing a product, various factors have to be taken into account, especially the income of the consumer. In order to attract the consumer a variety of pricing policies may be followed – often involving discounts. It is essential that price covers variable costs, but the higher the price the lower demand is likely to be. There are several difficulties in setting the best price. Both too low a price and too high a price will fail to maximise revenue. In this chapter we will discuss:

▶ factors to consider when setting price
▶ types of pricing policy
▶ discounts

Factors to consider when setting price

If a loss is to be avoided, the price of a product should cover the variable costs incurred in making it. The variable costs include direct labour, direct material and direct overheads. Price setting should not be done in isolation, though, since the consumer will often have other companies' products to compare. The greater the choice of products the greater the elasticity of demand. (See chapter 2 on elasticity). When setting price the marketing department needs to consider:

1. Likely contribution to fixed costs made by the sale of one product.

2. Predicted sales.

3. Competitors' strategies – if the market is price-sensitive it is important that the price is not set too high.

4. Image of the product – too low a price may suggest that the product is of poor quality.

5. Stock levels – a high level of stock could result in a deliberately low price in order to clear the product from the stockrooms.

6. Stage of the product life cycle – for a newly introduced product, an initial low price may be set in order to break into the market.

7. Image of the company – if the seller's reputation is as a low price retailer/producer then a high price product will arouse suspicion. Woolworths' would find it difficult to sell high-priced products for this reason.

Problems in price-setting

With the range of considerations outlined above, it is clear there are problems for the price-setter. These include:

(a) Initial price setting – if the price is set too low, it will be difficult to raise it later.

(b) If competitors drop their prices, what should the reaction be?

(c) How to estimate the reaction of the consumer to the price and subsequent price changes. To assess this, market research may be carried out but that may be unreliable owing to size of sample, accuracy of responses and changes in the competitive environment. A consumer may say he will buy more if you drop the price but when you do – and the competition follows suit – the consumer simply switches away from your (cheaper) product to the (even cheaper) product of your competitor.

(d) Sometimes products are bought in combination. Each product in the set may have different profit margins and so a price change in the overall product may eat into the individual profits. For example, imagine a computer sold for £1,000 complete with £600 worth of software. This is compared to another computer which offers exactly the same but without the software. If the price differential is £100 then the consumer is paying £100 for the privilege of having the extra software. If the price of the 'with software' computer is now dropped to £950 then – from the consumer's point of view – he is paying an extra £50 for the software. If the consumer would be unable to buy the software separately for less than £600, he would be receiving £600 worth of software for an extra £50. If the retailer is having to pay £100 for the software then on the software alone he is making a £50 loss (the price differential) but he is gaining a sale. The profit from the sale offsets the loss on the software.

(e) If the product is distributed via a retailer, the retailer may have a fixed mark-up of £1.00 per item. If you now cut your price *but* still have to pay the retailer the same amount as before, then the reduction in price comes directly off your element of the price.

Types of pricing policy

Skimming
Skimming means charging a high price for a new product. The demand for such a product is likely to be inelastic in the short run. Over a period of time, once competitors appear on the scene, the product's price may fall. Typical examples are pocket calculators, videos and personal computers. The high initial price may be necessary to cover the high cost of research and development.

Penetration
The price is set low for a new product to enable the company to break into the market. As popularity increases, the price may be raised.

The diagram on page 110 shows both penetration and skimming. Over a period of time the price will change once a market share has been gained (penetration) or initial costs have been covered (skimming).

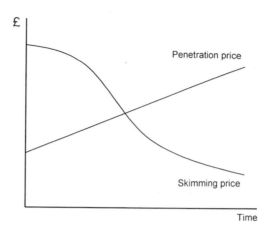

Figure 27. Penetration and skimming pricing.

Loss leaders

These are products sold at a price below cost. The idea is to attract the consumer into the shop to buy the product, for example baked beans for 20p, and then while there, it is hoped the consumer will go on to buy a host of other products. Thus a restaurant may sell coffee at 4p a cup to the first three customers after 5 pm. The consumers come in and have the coffee – and then they may decide to buy a meal since it is almost dinner time. Also the restaurateur will make sure the customer sits in the window to act as an advertisement to attract new customers. (Few people will enter a restaurant that appears empty.)

Economic price

This is the lowest price that may be charged if the costs are to be covered. To set an economic price, we need precise data about the costs of making each individual product. For every product made, we should be able to calculate the exact costs of production.

Market price

The market price is the price that people expect to pay. One example is private tuition. In places such as Oxford and Cambridge, a tutorial college is expected to charge about £30 an hour. Anything less than that (or well in excess of) is viewed by customers with suspicion.

Discounts

Discounts are offered to encourage increased/repeat purchases. There are five main types of discount:

Quantity discount
Typically this would be 'buy two, get one free' offers.

Trade discount
This is offered to people trading in the same sector. Thus a school may be able to receive an 'educational discount' on the purchase of a computer, or a landscape gardener will receive a discount from a garden centre on plants purchased due to the greater quantity purchased than the average private consumer.

Seasonal discount
The purpose of a seasonal discount is to increase demand at special times of the year/month/week/day. An example is the promotion of 'off-peak' railway tickets.

Cash discount
The receipt of cash, instead of having to wait for payment on invoice, will benefit the seller, not least in terms of cash flow. To encourage customers to pay with cash, a discount may be offered for example '5% reduction in sale price if cash is paid'.

Geographical discounts
A discount may be offered in relation to the distance from the supply base. An example would be new car delivery; the greater the distance away, the greater the discount. This would be to encourage sales in places that may be unaware of the retailer.

Tutorial: helping you learn

Progress test

1. State three types of price.

2. Draw the following types of pricing policy:

    (a) skimming
    (b) penetration.

3. What is the link between price and elasticity?

Discussion point

Is price the most important element in the marketing mix?

Practical assignment

There are ten types of price not covered in this chapter. Find out the meaning of each. Give an example of a product that may be priced in each of these ways.

1. psychological price
2. opportunity price
3. non-discriminatory price
4. uniform delivery price
5. basic point pricing
6. distorted price
7. dumping
8. double pricing
9. controlled price
10. guaranteed price.

Study/revision tip

If price rises then demand will tend to fall. If demand rises (for reasons not connected to price) then price is likely to rise too. The first event is referred to as contraction of demand, the second to a shift in demand.

16

Product Mix

One-minute summary – The product mix refers to the range of products offered by a firm. When deciding the range, the individual contribution of each product is taken into account, as well as likely demand for the product and factors such as substitutes available from competitors. Firms will also consider the rate of return in the period over a particular time period; some products will be expected to break even within a short period – perhaps because of the high cash outflows of investment. Likely return is a key factor in new product development. In this chapter we will discuss:

▶ pre-production considerations
▶ new product development process
▶ test marketing
▶ product failure
▶ product mix

Pre-production considerations

Before deciding whether to develop a new product, a number of internal and external factors have to be considered.

Internal factors

1. The existing product range – will the new product cannibalise existing sales?

2. Resources available versus resources needed.

3. The current image of the business – does the new product add to or complement the existing image?

4. Existing capacity – does the company have space for the new product?

5. Internal financial criteria – the likely return on the product per year and overall.

6. Probable payback period – how long before the initial investment is realised?

External factors
This new product will take time to develop and time to make a return on the capital investment. The main external factors affecting demand include:

(a) Competitors – do they exist now/will they exist when the product is launched?

(b) Strengths and weaknesses of the competitors?

(c) Likely changes in the economy that may affect demand such as interest rates, tax rates, public expenditure cut-backs.

(d) Efficiency and accuracy of the marketing strategy.

The new product development process

Every new product will go through a screening process before launch. The screening will consider:

1. Resources needed to make and market this product.
2. Likely payback time (see above).
3. Likely competition, and their reactions to the launch of this product.

When the questions posed above have been answered to the satisfaction of the financiers, the new product idea changes into the product concept. At this stage the financiers will test:

(a) The benefits of the product to the company in qualitative and quantitative terms.

(b) The position of the product in comparisons with its rivals.

(c) The market itself – is it ready for this product?

If the product proves to be satisfactory, then the finance *may* be forthcoming. Financiers may well have other products to consider, perhaps with fewer risks. The financiers may be cautious investors, unwilling to take risks – or at least preferring a near-guaranteed gain, albeit small, compared to the chance of a higher return (and a greater chance of failure).

The product then moves to the design stage. When designing a product the following factors are considered:

1. Legislation relating to safety and product liability.

2. Source of materials – do they have to be from the host country to fit in with the marketing image ('Made in Britain')?

3. The performance of the product – quality, durability, reliability, ease of operation and maintenance.

4. Costs of production – these to include the fixed element (apportioned to the product) as well as the variable costs.

5. Environmental and social considerations – is the product made with recyclable material? Or will the manufacturing process lead to a diminishing of scarce non-renewable resources?

6. Likely response of competitors.

7. Demand of the consumer (and hence market orientation – making what the consumer is identified as wanting).

Test marketing

The next stage is test marketing. The test market must:

1. be representative of the market as a whole

2. be typical in terms of distributive outlets and per capita income

3. have a previous good record as a test area (for the same sort of product market)

4. have advertising media that will co-operate.

Problems with test markets

The major problem with testing a product in a real market is that competitors will see what you are doing! Thus if the main selling point of your product is a low price, competitors may then decide to drop their own prices (in advance of your main launch), or create the impression in the mind of the consumer that low price equates with low quality.

Other problems concern selecting the market and the length of time for testing. At best a test market represents the whole population at that moment in time. If your product is launched nationally six months later, the demand may have changed. Consumers are fickle and fashion is such that if your product is deemed 'unfashionable' after the test market period has long ended, then the product will flop.

Product failure

Despite intensive in-house testing, consumer panels, test marketing and thorough appraisal, a product may still fail. The following are typical reasons:

(a) The test market period was too short. Conditions of demand changed soon after (e.g. the government cut income tax) meaning the product was no longer as popular.

(b) The data from the test marketing was incorrect and/or wrongly interpreted.

(c) After a six-month period of use it was found that the product became dangerous, for example, the paint wore off exposing a toxic surface underneath or the machine overheated when left on for 4 months continuously when the testing period only covered three months.

(d) Competitors, having realised the new product's strengths, redeveloped their own product and consolidated their market position before launch. This applies particularly to software where competitors will offer free upgrades to existing products to ensure a newer package does not become the preferred choice.

(e) Although production times and costs had been estimated, the workforce chose now to push for higher wages; this increased the unit labour costs. Worse still, to support their claim the work force may go on strike therefore delaying production times and further escalating costs. This poor industrial relations will be written about in the main press, characterising the company as a tyrant employer and as a result sales bomb.

Product mix

Even if the product does succeed, it may just be one product within a range of products. The term 'product mix' refers to the range of products the company offers. Ideally the mix will be made up of a variety of products at different stages of their own product life cycles. As one product's sales decline, another product is in the growth stage.

When evaluating the spread of products the producer will consider:

1. The individual contribution made by each product. (Contribution is selling price less variable costs. Thus the unit

contribution multiplied by the total output equals total contribution.)

2. Forecast buying habits of the population. Maybe it is time to increase production of one product and distance yourself from another.

3. Competitors' strategies.

4. Production costs. One product is now a lot more expensive to produce than originally owing to the rise in price of a particular essential raw material.

Tutorial: helping you learn

Progress questions
1. Outline three main reasons why a product may fail.

2. What are the main problems associated with test marketing?

3. What is considered when designing a product?

Discussion point
What type of events is it almost impossible to plan for when launching a new product?

Practical assignment
Research the Boston Matrix. Select products currently in existence that would fit into each of the Boston segments.

Study/revision tip
A product may succeed or fail owing to both internal and external events. External events include changes in the economy as well as global political events. The external environments (social, legal, economic, political and technological) are all intertwined.

17

Non-Financial Ratios

One-minute summary – The trouble with financial ratios is that they only assess the business in a quantitative sense. A qualitative analysis is also needed. Unless the background to the figures is understood, it is difficult to reach sound decisions for the future. A business is not just about the figures of profit and loss. The managers need to understand all the contributory factors. Have profits fallen because of a rise in staff absenteeism, resulting in a fall in productivity? Are expenses so high because salesmen have been allocated to the wrong territories? Or it is costing too much per order in terms of sales expenses? Non-financial ratios seek to look behind the balance sheet and profit and loss account, and delve into the *qualitative* side of the business. In this chapter we will discuss:

▶ work force ratios
▶ sales force ratios
▶ the product's ratios

Work force ratios

Labour turnover

$$\frac{\text{number of separations during a period}}{\text{average number employed during a period}} \times 100$$

This ratio measures annual labour turnover. It is not perfect, though, because it includes the total 'number of separations', in other words those that are unavoidable. For example, someone may leave work because his or her partner is desperately ill, or out of a desire to move away from the area. It's of little use to design personnel policy based on a ratio that may be giving the wrong signals. A better ratio would be one without the unavoidable separations:

$$\frac{\text{number leaving minus unavoidable separations}}{\text{average number employed}} \times 100$$

The labour turnover ratio is an indicator of unhappiness within the organisation. Follow-up information is needed, in particular that gleaned from an 'exit interview'. The policy of inviting every leaving employee to an interview where they are asked to report the main reasons for their departure can show a trend which can be remedied by appropriate action.

A high labour turnover is expensive for a firm. It will lead to costs associated with:

1. recruitment
2. lost production or fall in service while the post is unfilled
3. a poor image
4. discontinuity with customers as sales personnel are continually leaving
5. costs of training newcomers
6. break-up of work groups
7. overtime payments to those on cover until a replacement is found.

Labour stability index

$$\frac{\text{employees with at least one year's service}}{\text{number of employees employed one year ago}}$$

As the name suggests, this ratio measures the stability of the workforce. Again, a low labour turnover helps to foster teamwork and continuity. On the other hand, if no one leaves at all, the result may be stagnation – a workforce without challenge, change, and bereft of new ideas and motivation.

Ratios from an employees' attitude survey

1. % of employees happy with management style.

2. % of employees happy with the performance of the company
3. % of requests for a change in job compared to % of requests last year
4. % of complaints this year compared to last year

The employee attitude survey may not tell you about people thinking of leaving, but it will show you the degree of motivation among the workforce. Again, this may not directly affect productivity, especially if pay is linked to productivity, but a demotivated workforce is more likely to resist change and less likely to welcome new training and new procedures. The employee attitude survey can highlight potential problems for the future.

Industrial action
1. number of days lost through industrial action: number of days lost last year
2. output lost through work to rule/overtime ban this year : last year
3. number of times ACAS (Advisory, Conciliatory and Arbitration Service) called in
4. % of complaints made to arbitration committee upheld.

The fewer days lost through industrial action, the better industrial relations would seem. One ratio by itself is not sufficient. Workers may not go on strike for fear of losing their job, and not being able to afford a loss of pay. However, they may still be unhappy with management and may express that unhappiness by not working any overtime or by working very slowly.

This same workforce is likely to be obstructive and refuse to take part in any joint management/workers committees. It is important to find out why this should be, and then take necessary remedial action.

Sales force ratios

The wages of the sales force make up one of the major elements of marketing expenditure. First, it may be very expensive to sell the goods. Second, the information derived from the sales force may be late, out of date or inaccurate. If the salesman is not wholly enthusiastic about his job, he may be late in submitting useful information to his employers – and his dissatisfaction may show through when he is trying to sell the product.

The sales force may also be badly organised, faced with a large amount of travelling per day, per person. With the growth of the customer base, it might make more sense to reallocate the sales territories and try and ensure that each salesman's client list is actually a cluster of customers on the map, so that travelling time and costs are minimised. It might be better to allocate existing customers to newer salesman and new customers to those who are more experienced. It could be that one particular salesman inevitably feels he has to spend the night when he sees certain customers – and bill his employers accordingly.

Some salesmen make more calls than others and have a higher conversion rate. Using sales force ratios will help managers build up information on which to base merit awards and identify worthwhile areas for training.

The product's ratios

The balance sheet and trading and profit and loss account show the profits and the sales revenue. What they do not show is the sales per product, the stage of the product life cycle or the degree of market share.

For example, the sales revenue figure does not tell you whether a change from the prior year is the result of an increase in volume, price or both. No account is taken of the influence of competitors; perhaps sales rose in a particular week because a major competitor raised its prices.

The key product ratios to calculate are:

1. market share – as a trend against the total market
2. aggregate market share from a range of products
3. volume figures.

From these figures one can extrapolate a trend and then make predictions on volume sales. These predictions in turn may be built into cash flow forecasts.

Year on year sales revenue comparisons will need further analysis before variance analysis can be carried out. Key factors would include the volumes and prices of a range of products. Variance analysis looks at the differences between actual and budgeted figures and seeks to suggest reasons why the figures may differ.

Tutorial: helping you learn

Progress questions
1. State two ratios for labour turnover.

2. State one ratio that measures industrial action.

3. What are the main costs associated with a high labour turnover?

Discussion point
Suppose that, after a price drop, market share increases. Would it be a good idea to drop prices even further?

Practical assignment
Select any business and try to calculate its key ratios for profitability. Also, plot the trend figures for its sales revenue, gross and net profit. On the same graph, plot days lost through industrial action and output figures. Measure the degree of correlation between the trend lines.

Study/revision tip
How people respond to questionnaires may change according to mood. Unlike financial ratios, attitudes may change from day to day.

18

Human Resource Management in the Third Millennium

One-minute overview – As the new millennium has only just begun, it seems appropriate to consider areas of human resource management that may develop further as the millennium progresses. In this chapter we will discuss:

▶ motivation through the working environment
▶ workplace norms
▶ China
▶ dealing with trade unions
▶ the minimum wage
▶ changes to come in employment law
▶ stress at work

Motivation through the working environment

The human relations theorist, Herzberg, concluded that the working environment was a demotivator unless it reached a required standard. *Feng shui* is being used by some companies to transform the office environment into a positive motivator. According to Huw Griffiths and Kate Lord – leading *feng shui* consultants – *feng shui* is based upon unchanging natural characteristics and laws. It is derived from strict observation of the conditions, compass directions, mathematics, and *i'ching*. This, when correctly computed, indicates the flow of *ch'i* (energy), its qualities, and the general character of the space being evaluated.

It is hoped that an office with positive energy qualities will motivate staff, increase customers' willingness to buy and hence increase sales as well as staff productivity.

Workplace norms

In his book *The Great Disruption; Human Nature and the reconstitution of Social Order*, Francis Fukuyama stresses the need for social connectedness to turn ideas into wealth. Impersonal information shared via the internet fails to build respect and trust. According to Charles Handy:

> 'Where will we find our social connectedness in the future and who will set our norms and the rules? My guess is that, as ever, the workplace, however virtual it may be, will always be a key community whose norms will ripple out into society for good or ill ...'

This gives business a responsibility as an agent for stability and/or an agent for change in society.

China

China has a population of 1.2 billion, nearly 20% of the world's population. The economic growth rate in China in 1998 was 7.8%. Capital investment by the state has increased by 28%. Management style has to develop at a similar rate to maximise the opportunities that this growth will bring.

China lacks companies with a global presence. China's business empire used to be controlled by the military which put an emphasis on employment rather than productivity. The workforce is uncompetitive but the low wages are attracting inward investment.

Chinese management outside of China is built on:

1. close family ties
2. sharp commercial acumen
3. control over costs
4. cautious finance

Modern management is about decentralisation, downsizing, and democratic entrepreneurship. Once China encapsulates these basics, then – with a willing population and increased state spending – its economy will be set to challenge the West as no economy, including that of Japan, has done before.

Dealing with trade unions

Trade unions have modernised. They have their own web sites; their leaders wear expensive business suits; they discuss 'pan-European action' and urge closer economic, social and political ties with Europe. The TUC has formed an 'organising academy' that trains young activists in employment law, negotiating tactics, business economics and communication skills.

In dealing with trade unions in the third millennium it will be even more important:

1. not to underestimate their intellectual power

2. to assess the relationship between the leaders of the union and the grass roots

3. to know about union internal politics as well as the faces, names and nature of the local union representatives

4. to know your own limitations, in other words the maximum the company will offer as well as the minimum that the unions will accept

5. to be aware of European as well as UK labour laws.

Trade unions are slowly being divorced from the Labour party (the Labour government). To survive, they have not only become more appealing to potential members but also more capable of meeting management on equal intellectual terms.

The talk now is of partnership – not only with management – but also with government.

The minimum wage

Despite dire warnings from the Conservatives, the minimum wage has not so far led to increased unemployment, rampaging inflation or a fall in international competitiveness.

The Confederation of British Industry issued a report in autumn 1999 giving 'qualified support' to the minimum wage. The key points were:

1. Not much evidence of a significant impact on employment or unemployment.

2. No noticeable blip upwards in average earnings.

3. The impact on inflation was 'unlikely to be significant'.

4. The minimum wage has made some impact on wage differentials leading to higher rates for other workers and not just the low paid, but this only applies to 13 per cent of companies.

5. The introduction of a lower £3 an hour development rate for 18-21 year olds has proved effective for small companies.

6. The exemption of under-18 year olds from any minimum wage has proved 'useful and valuable' to employers.

7. Some companies have modernised work practices by making staff more multi-skilled. They rotate them more between jobs to offset the cost of the minimum wage

With trade unions pressing for a broadening of the categories covered by the minimum wage, wages are likely to rise somewhat ahead of inflation. Differentials will be further eroded and there may come a time when the warnings, mentioned above, come true. If this should happen, management will have to plan for the increase in labour costs without losing competitiveness.

Changes in the law to come

The Part-time Work Directive

On the 15th December 1997 the EU Directive on part-time work was adopted. Under the directive part-timers are entitled to pro rata benefits and member states are required to introduce measures to encourage part-time work.

The UK has two years from the date of adoption of the extension of the directive to the UK (7 April 1998) to implement it.

The Disability Rights Commission Act 1999

This Act received Royal Assent on 27 July 1999. It enables the Secretary of State to set up a Disability Rights Commission (DRC) with similar powers to those of the Equal Opportunities Commission and the Commission for Racial Equality. The DRC will be operational by April 2000.

The aims of the Disability Rights Commission are to:

1. work towards eliminating discrimination against disabled people

2. promote equal opportunities for disabled people

3. provide information and advice particularly to disabled people, employers and service providers

4. prepare codes of practice and encourage good practice

5. keep the working of the 1995 Act under review

6. investigate discrimination and ensure compliance with the law

7. arrange for a conciliation service between service providers and disabled people to help resolve disputes concerning access to goods and services.

The Human Rights Act 1998

The Human Rights Act of 1998 received Royal Assent on 9 November 1998. It incorporates the European Convention on Human Rights into UK law. It will come fully into force on 2 October 2000. Of particular interest are the right to privacy (Article 8) and the right to form and join a trade union (Article 9).

Stress at work

Cases brought against management for neglect are likely to increase. An employer has a duty of care towards employees and as stress-related illnesses increase, so employees will increasingly seek compensation from their employers.

In September 1999 Gee Publishing produced a report concerning stress at work. It concluded that:

1. Stress is now the number one reason behind sickness from work – overtaking the common cold as the biggest cause of absence.

2. One third of employers are now providing stress counselling for employees because they are increasingly worried about the impact the problem will have on their business. Not only is there the possibility of litigation, absenteeism and mistakes but highly stressed workers may become involved in fights or, even worse, attack customers verbally or physically.

Tutorial: helping you learn

Progress test

1. Which theorist may have his work contradicted by *feng shui*?

2. Name one piece of legislation yet to come into force that will affect employees at work.

3. Why is stress at work becoming a bigger problem today?

Discussion points

'Getting things done is most certainly about good people management skills and there isn't a senior management executive who doesn't believe that, or feel that they are doing it. However the increasing pressures of business life make these good intentions difficult to execute in the hustle and bustle of everyday corporate life ...' Professor Cary Cooper, Pro-Vice Chancellor, UMIST.

What steps can HRM take to develop these skills?

Practical assignments

1. 'The government is helping people into work through the New Deal, the UK's largest ever employment programme, and by making work pay through the Working Families Tax Credit and the new national minimum wage ...' *Labour Party Annual Report*, 1998/9.

    Evaluate the impact of these three policies on recruitment policies in (i) a small business and (ii) a large business.

2. Many companies publish their HRM policies. Contact two companies of your choice and compare their HRM policies in particular on:

    (a) grievances
    (b) employment
    (c) redundancies
    (d) pay

3. In what ways has European legislation changed the employment rights of an employee?

Study/revision tip

If you are doing part-time work, ask what changes have been made in employment rights and practices since you started. Ask also if there are any changes due to come in. In this way you will be able to relate changes in the workplace to your outside work.

19

Critical Path Analysis

One-minute summary – Critical path analysis is part of network analysis. A network diagram is constructed to show the relationships between different tasks/activities. These relationships are plotted in sequence. By plotting such activities, we can see which ones have to be completed before subsequent activities are begun. Carrying out critical path analysis enables us to allocate time and resources to maximise efficiency and minimise down time. In this chapter we will discuss:

▶ drawing a simple network
▶ features of a network
▶ non-critical activities
▶ EST (earliest start time) and LFT (latest finishing time)

Drawing a simple network

A network shows the interrelationship of various activities. Figure 29 will serve as an illustration.

Activity	Time taken (hours)	Order
A	1	This is the start activity. It is followed by others
B	2	This activity occurs directly after A.
C	1	This activity occurs directly after A. (Note: B and C occur directly after A. Thus they start at the same time and rely on the completion of A before they can commence).
D	3	This activity follows B. (Note: it does not follow C, which is further proof that B and C follow different paths).
E	1	This activity follows C.
F	1	This activity follows E.
G	2	This activity follows D and F. (This means activities D and F 'meet' at G. Thus if either D or F is late in completion, G cannot start. If D and F finish at different times then there will be spare time 'float' where resources are not being used unless they are transferable to another activity.

Figure 28. An activity list.

131

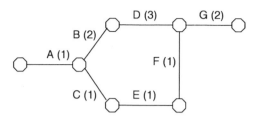

Figure 29. A simple network.

Explanations

1. The lines represent activities.

2. The circles show where one activity ends/begins. The circle is known as a node. Later we will see how this circle also contains EST (earliest start time) and LFT (latest finishing time).

3. The project is not completed until all the activities have finished.

4. The time for each activity is shown on the activity line.

Rules for drawing networks

1. There is only one entry and one exit point in each network.

2. The drawing is not to scale. The important point is clarity. Thus a long activity line does not denote a long activity time.

3. Wherever possible the lines should be straight – use a ruler!

4. The diagram should be read from left to right. In the example above we can see that the network starts with activity A and concludes with activity G.

5. Every activity has a preceding event (a circle) and a succeeding one. Remember – the line is the activity; the circle is the event.

6. No activity can be started until the previous activity(ies) has been completed.

7. All activities are part of the network. If they have nothing to do with it then they should not appear in the diagram.

Features of a network
The following diagrams show parts of any network. Representing activities/events by a network diagram is like learning a code. It is important that the rules of drawing the network and the codes used in illustrating activities/events are learned to enable the correct interpretation of questions/instructions.

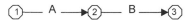

Figure 30. The features of a network. A must be completed before B is begun.

This shows that activity B cannot be started until activity A has been completed. Activity A's completion is shown by the drawing of the circle/even number 2. The numbers in the circles illustrate the order of events.

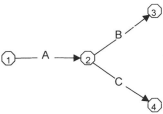

Figure 31. Features of a network. A must be completed before B or C is begun.

Activity A is completed at event 2. Until A is completed neither B nor C can be started. B and C start from the same point. B and C start at the same time, though it is important to note that this does not necessarily show that they *finish* at the same time.

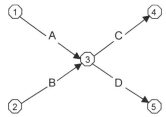

Figure 32. Features of a network. Simultaneous jobs.

Activity A and B are independent of each other. They may take different times to complete but until they are *both* completed event 3 cannot start. Event 3 leads to activities C and D. An event is simply a transition between activities. Thus if activity B takes longer than activity A (assuming they both start at the same time) there will be spare resources, while C and D are waiting for B to finish. These spare resources are known as float and are referred to as 'time'.

Non-critical activities

The total time for the project can be calculated by adding together the times of activities, but not for all of them – only for those on the critical path. The critical path is the longest route for the completion of all activities. Thus in the basic diagram above, the critical path is A, B, D, G. The time taken is $1 + 2 + 3 + 2 = 8$ hours.

▶ *Key point* – If any activity in the critical path is delayed then the project will take longer than was originally planned. If any of the other activities take longer than expected there may still be enough float to account for the extra time. Thus if E in the simple network diagram took 2 hours there would still be time, since activity G cannot start until A, B, and D are finished. A, B and D take 6 hours.

EST (earliest start time) and LFT (latest finishing time)

To understand these concepts, refer back to figure 29. It can be seen from the diagram that activity B could start (at the earliest) after 1 hour (as A takes 1 hour). Activity D could start after 3 hours (time for A and B to finish). Activity C could start after 1 hour and E could start after 2 hours.

Activity G could not start until D has finished, though so even though the time for A, C, E and F to finish is 4 hours, G must wait for D. thus G could not start for 6 hours. The earliest start time for G is therefore 6 hours.

The latest time for G to finish is 8 hours. Therefore the earliest time for any activity after G to start is 8 hours too.

This may be illustrated as follows:

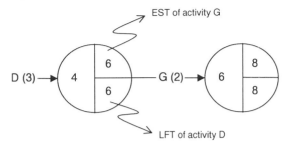

Figure 33. An extract from a network diagram showing earliest start time and earliest finish time.

In the above diagram we see an extract from the simple network diagram. The earliest start time for G has been found by adding activities A, B and D together.

Note that activity F takes 1 hour only. Thus activity F could start after 5 hours (and this is the latest finishing time of activity E). However, since A, C and E only take 3 hours, the earliest start time is 3 hours. So the node for activity F would look like this:

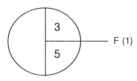

Figure 34. Further analysis of network diagram.

Thus we see that activity F has a different EST and LFT. The difference denoted the flexibility, or float, for F. It could take 2 hours longer.

LFT is found by working backwards from the final node thus:

LFT for D and F = 8 – 2 = 6

LFT for E = 8 – 2 – 1 = 5

LFT for C = 8 – 2 – 1 – 1 = 4

LFT for A = 1 (not 3). If A is late then B will be late, and so will D and G. Remember: in the critical path there is no float and no flexibility for lateness.

Tutorial: helping you learn

Progress test
1. What is a 'node'?

2. What does the term 'critical path' mean?

Discussion point
If it looks as though the activities in the critical path will be late, what steps could management take?

Practical assignment
Describe fully what is happening in the network diagram below. Calculate the EST, LFT and comment on the areas of float.

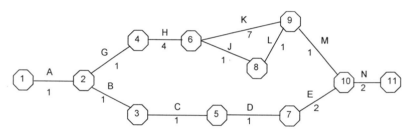

Figure 35. Network diagram illustrating float areas.

Study/revision tip
Make sure you learn the rules/codes before you start interpreting questions. You can check the accuracy of your diagram by trying to interpret the order of activities after the diagram has been drawn.

20

Europe and Business – 1

One-minute summary – The following three chapters deal with the impact of Europe on business, and vice versa. 'Europe' is a huge topic and worth a whole business studies book on its own since it has an increasing impact on both business and private life. The common agricultural policy, the fisheries policy, the social contract, the single currency, the EU budget and also food safety – all are featured in the next three chapters. Extensive references are given and practical assignments encourage further investigation. In this chapter we will discuss:

▶ the EU's social policy
▶ the EU and employment
▶ competition policy and state aids
▶ the EU and the US

The EU's social policy

The term 'social policy' covers all issues involving co-operation between member states. It covers social security, training and employment. Legislation includes measures affecting:

1. equal social security rights in member states

2. transfer of social security contributions

3. application of the principle of equal opportunities to old age pensions, social security and retirement benefits

4. disability issues and even combating racism and xenophobia.

Financing of the social policy

In the UK, social policy is financed by government sources as follows:

(a) revenue from the collection of taxes
(b) sale of nationalised industries (privatisation)
(c) revenue from the trading activities of government organisations
(d) borrowing (the PSBR, or public sector borrowing requirement).

As social policy expands, so the funds needed are greater. Where unemployment rises, so will spending, and there is likely to be a budget deficit. The government's revenues fall when fewer people work (income tax) and fewer firms make profits (corporation tax).

The dependency ratio refers to the number of people who do not work – children, students, pensioners, and unemployed – compared with those who do. As the dependency ratio grows, so must taxation and/or economic growth.

Social policy in Europe is financed with funds from the European Social Fund which pays for vocational training and retraining.

EU-financed initiatives have also been taken to:

1. assist the elderly ('the European year of solidarity between generations')

2. address the needs of disabled people (the European Disability Forum; exchange of best practice through the HELIOS programme)

3. promote public health issues (the Europe against AIDS and Europe against Cancer campaigns).

4. highlight unemployment (the 1993 Delors white paper, *Growth, Competitiveness and Employment*) which led to employment concerns being made a priority in other EU policies and the development and implementation of national action plans for employment.

The EU and employment

The employment policy is part of the social policy. These are the key issues:

Health and safety at work

Regarded as an important element in creating a 'level playing field' within the single market, common standards were adopted at the EU. They sought to protect workers from risks associated with a variety of dangerous chemicals, carcinogens, asbestos and noise.

In the UK the most controversial measure was the 1993 Working Time Directive; this placed a ceiling on the maximum average number of hours which an employer can require employees to work.

Equal treatment

Pay, equal access to employment, training and promotion as well as equal treatment under social security and pension schemes.

Labour law

The 1993 Maastricht Treaty contained a short 7-article Agreement on Social Policy. This was designed to implement the 1989 Social Charter and opened up the areas of social exclusion and management/ labour dialogue to action at the EU level.

The Agreement on Social Policy

With the change of government in 1997 in the UK, it was decided that the Agreement on Social Policy attached to the Maastricht Treaty should apply in the UK. Only 4 directives have been adopted under the agreement – directives on works councils, parental leave, an EU level framework agreement between Employers (UNICE, CEEP) and trade unions (ETUC) on part time work, and on the burden of proof in sex discrimination cases.

National Action Plans (NAPs) for employment

A new employment title is included in the Amsterdam Treaty with the aim of establishing a co-ordinated employment strategy and promoting a skilled, adaptable work force.

Worker consultation at national level

The Works Councils Directive applies to multinationals and larger sized companies.

Competition policy and state aids

The aim of EU competition policy is to guarantee an undistorted Single Market. Without an active competition policy, consumers would not enjoy the full benefits of a healthy, competitive EU market meaning a wider choice of goods and services available at the lowest possible prices.

EU competition policy has three main objectives:

1. to prevent companies from entering into price-fixing and market-sharing agreement

2. to prevent anti-competitive practices which may result in market power being concentrated in monopoly, duopoly or oligopoly. A business that is a monopoly may make customers pay unfairly high prices or squeeze out smaller competitors through predatory pricing. Equally, dominant positions can be abused through distribution arrangements such as exclusive dealerships or imposed customer 'loyalty' contracts

3. to prevent national governments from distorting competition in the community by favouring national companies.

Key legislation in the Treaty of Rome

▶ *Article 85* – 'The following shall be prohibited as incompatible with the common market: all agreement between undertakings, decision by association of undertakings and concerted practices which may affect trade between member states and which have as their object or effect the prevention, restriction or distortion of competition within the common market.'

▶ *Article 86* – 'Any abuse by one or more undertakings of a dominant position within the common market or in a substantial part of it shall be prohibited as incompatible with the common market in so far as it may affect trade within member states.'

The EU and the US

The European Union has close links with the United States.

Economic links
The EU and the US are each other's major commercial partners, with more than 350 billion ecu (£230 bn) of goods and services traded. The EU is the major source of inward investment to the US and vice versa.

Political links
The US president, the presidency of the EU Council of Ministers and the president of the European Commission now meet every six months.

Personal links
One of the strongest elements in the relationship is the daily contact between families, businessmen, students, universities and others.

Common values
▶ *Free Trade* – Both the EU and the US advocate free trade. Both supported the Uruguay Round deal which reduced tariffs, and both supported stronger powers for the World Trade Organisation (the successor to GATT – General Agreement on Tariffs and Trade).

▶ *Global challenges* – The EU and the US have co-operated on action against international crime and the drugs trade.

Tutorial: helping you learn

Progress questions
1. What are the three objectives of European competition policy?

2. Outline three aspects of the Social Chapter.

3. What is in Article 85 and Article 86 of the Treaty of Rome?

Discussion point

In 1999 British beef was still banned by France. French beef was not, however, banned from the UK. Were both sides right?

Practical assignment

1. Compare European and UK competition policy in the following areas:

    (a) restrictive agreements
    (b) abuse of monopoly power
    (c) mergers

2. Outline the main areas covered by the Social Chapter and assess the possible impact on employment security and international competitiveness. You may choose to refer to the Social Chapter:
    http://www.economics.tcd.ie/amtthews/EurEcon/Lectures/Lecture%2011/tsld008.htm
    http://www.echo.lu/legal/en/treaties/ec/social.html
    http://ds.dial.pipex.com/geoff.riley/social.htm
    http://www.eubusiness.com/social/socialbr.htm

3. How might the common agricultural policy be reformed and what would the effects be on UK business? You may choose to refer to:
    http://www.minlnv.nl/international/policy/inta/notutie.htm
    http://www.wsws.org/articles/1999/mar1999/cap-m05.shtml
    http://europe.eu.int/pol/agr/instcapen.htm
    http://www1.europarl.eu.int/dg4/factsheets/en/412.htm

Study/revision tip

Many of the 'changes' brought about by the Social Chapter were not changes at all, since workers were already protected in the UK by existing legislation.

21

Europe and Business – 2

One-minute summary – In recent years a major source of controversy in the UK has been over the contributions made by the UK to the EU budget – not only the size of the budget but the actual and proposed areas of expenditure. In addition to the budget, controversy raged in 1999 over food and its safety. In this chapter we will discuss:

▶ the EU budget
▶ the UK and the EU budget
▶ how the EU budget is spent
▶ consumer policy and food safety
▶ fraud
▶ consumer policy
▶ food safety

The EU budget

The general budget of the European Union is currently ECU 85 billion per year (over £55 billion). Although this is a large sum in absolute terms, it represents slightly over 1% of EU GNP. By contrast, domestic public spending represents over 40% of UK GNP.

Revenue sources
The sources of revenue for the EU budget are:

VAT-based contributions – 37% in 1999
This is calculated by applying a national rate of VAT (value added tax) to an identical range of goods and services in each member state.

GNP-based contributions – 45%
The cost of financing the difference between the revenue raised by the other three 'own resources' and the total budget is allocated among member states in proportion to their gross national product (GNP).

Customs duties – 15%
Duties are levied on imports into the EU. The European Community is one territory for customs purposes. The rates of duty agreed at EU level apply at external frontiers. Member states deduct 10% to cover collection costs.

Remainder – 3%
The balance comes from agricultural and sugar levies charged on products imported to the EU from third countries, from bank interest, reserves and from taxes paid by employees of the EU institutions.

The UK and the EU budget

The calculations of the UK's net contribution follow the following procedure. The UK pays:

1. customs tariffs (directly to the EU)
2. agricultural levies (directly to the EU)
3. VAT contribution (according to the rate set by the Council)
4. direct UK government contribution (this is the GNP elements).

These four are added together and then the administration costs in collecting (a) and (b) are subtracted. This equals 'gross contribution'.

From this the following items are subtracted:

(a) the amount due to the UK for agricultural support (from the Intervention Board)
(b) Structural Fund payments.

The resulting figure represents the UK's net contribution/benefit.

How the EU budget is spent

European Union spending is split as follows:

1. administration
2. structural funds
3. education/youth
4. energy
5. research and development
6. transport
7. FEOGA. The European Agricultural Guidance and Guarantee Fund is usually known as FEOGA, the initials of the French name for the Fund. This is easily the largest item, approximately 60% of the total.

Fraud

A new, independent EU anti-fraud office was established in July 1999 (replacing the Commission's anti-fraud co-ordination unit UCLAF). It is backed by confidential anti-fraud hotlines across the EU. Furthermore, an independent watchdog institution – the Court of Auditors is responsible for making sure that EU budgetary rules are respected.

An independent report in September 1999 condemned the European Commission's management of public money. It studied how it paid its 16,000 civil servants, awarded contracts and granted subsidies – and concluded that its management was poor. The report offered a list of 90 recommendations, including the appointment of an EU 'prosecutor' with powers to investigate offences committed by EU officials.

However the report has been widely criticised for its over-reliance on external advisors, insufficient control of particularly vulnerable complex funds which make up 80% of the budget, and ineffective personnel policies.

EU consumer policy

The most important legislative measures are those adopted as part of the single market. Among the measures already in force are directives covering:

1. price indications on foodstuffs and non-food products
2. misleading advertising, distance selling and consumer credit
3. unfair terms in consumer contracts
4. the purchase of package tours and time shares.

Other consumer policies with an impact on consumer activities are:

(a) The common agricultural policy (CAP), particularly given the direct effects of support mechanisms on prices paid at the farm gate for many commodities. Other agricultural rules govern the labelling of meat, fruit and vegetables as well as wines and spirits. CAP quality control requirements also apply to a wide range of produce.

(b) Product safety standards have been developed by standards bodies at European level and are incorporated in EU legislation.

(c) Environment policy has a broader impact on such issues as air and water quality as well as the use of genetically modified organisms.

EU food safety

On the basis of its 1997 documents *Consumer Health and Food Safety* and *The General Principles of Food Law in the European Union*, the foundations have been laid for an EU approach to food safety issues. These foundations reflect two general principles:

1. Decision-making needs to be based on quality scientific advice that is broadly accepted as being independent.

2. Responsibility for legislation should be separate from that for inspection. There should be greater transparency and better access to information, both in the decision-making process and for inspection measures.

Tutorial: helping you learn

Progress questions
1. Where do the funds for the EU budget come from?

2. What is the money spent on?

3. What is the legal procedure if a member state imposes a ban on imports from another member state?

Discussion point
If the UK withdrew from the EU, what would be the effect on the Union's budget?

Practical assignments
1. Mrs Thatcher's position on budget contributions was that Britain paid too much and received too little. In hindsight, was the position of the former Conservative leader correct? You could start at this web site:

   http://news.bbc.co.uk/hi/english/business/theeconomy/news-id303000/303439.stm

2. Outline the current legislation in the EU on food and employment. You could refer to the following web sites:

   http://www.fst.rdg.ac.uk/foodlaw/eu/98a.htm
   http://www.fst.rdg.ac.uk/foodlaw/eu/news.htm
   http://www.emplaw.co.uk/free/data/034011.htm
   http://www.emplaw.co.uk/free/data/034006.htm
   http://www.foodexplorer.com/manu/industry/Fi02851.htm
   http://www.gene.ch/gentech/1997/Jul-Aug/msg00441.html
   http://www.hoyre.no/1997/notatutred/eduledig.html
   http://www.eubusiness.com/employ/981127co.htm

http://www.hrz.uni-giessen.de/fb03/seminar/online/europa99/text2.htm

3. Outline the role of the European Commission. You could refer to:

http://europa.eu.int/comm/index.htm

4. What key issues face Europe in the 21st century? See the following web site:

http://news.bbc.co.uk/hi/english/events/euros%5F99/europe/newsid%5F358000/358819.stm

5. According to an Electronic Telegraph article, the Institute of Directors wants a reduction of the tax burden. On the Institute of Directors web site they say the government must improve the climate for business. This is to be done through the budget:

http://www.telegraph.co.uk:80/et?ac=000696345546861&rtmo=faaNvYrs&atmo=99999999&pg=/et/00/1/17/cniod17.html

Outline the following:

(a) How the UK government may improve the climate for business.
(b) How the EU aims to improve the European economic climate.
(c) The key components in the EU/UK budgets.

6. Rumours circulate that the European Commission are still aiming at European tax harmonisation. Argue the case for and against tax harmonisation in Europe.

Study/revision tip
Consumer safety in Europe is represented by current UK consumer legislation.

22

Europe and Business – 3

One-minute summary – The debate over the single currency once more dominates the UK political scene. 'Europe' is probably the major area of division between and within the UK political parties. On 1 January 1999 Europe (minus the UK) signed up to a single currency. There will be a referendum in the UK 'one day soon' when the electorate will decide whether they wish to sign up. It is not clear whether the single currency would be of benefit whether to consumers, UK firms or to the UK economy. Certain convergence criteria have to be met – and it is unclear whether the pursuit of such criteria would result in all of Europe being at the same stage when the criteria are met. In this chapter we will discuss:

► the European convergence criteria
► the arguments for a single currency
► the arguments against a single currency
► the common fisheries policy

European convergence criteria

Before the UK joins the single currency it must meet certain convergence criteria set out in the Maastricht treaty:

1. Consumer price inflation must not exceed that of the three best-performing countries by more than 1.5%.

2. Interest rates on long-term government securities must not be more than 2% above those in the three best-performing member states.

3. The financial position must be sustainable. The general government deficit should be at or below the reference value of 3% of GDP. If not, it should have declined substantially and continuously; either it should have reached a level close to the reference value, or the excess over the reference value should be temporary and exceptional. The gross debt of general government should be at or below 60% of GDP; if not, the debt ratio should be sufficiently diminishing and approaching the 60% reference value at a satisfactory pace.

4. The exchange rate criterion is that the currency must have remained within the normal fluctuation margins of the ERM for two years without a realignment by the member state in question.

(Source: IMF 1996.)

There are two key doubts about this policy:

(a) Are these the right criteria?
(b) What happens after joining – will the criteria still be enforced?

Labour's five economic tests for joining the single currency
These questions have led the Labour government to detail five economic tests needed before it recommends to the British voters that the UK enters a single currency:

1. There must be a convergence of economic cycles – and this must be sustainable.

2. There must be sufficient flexibility to cope with economic change such as those that exist within the labour and product markets.

3. The overall impact of EMU must be good for investment.

4. It must be good for employment.

5.　It must be good for the financial services industry.

The arguments for a single currency

Firstly a caveat. The arguments for and against a single European currency are well covered in all economics/business studies textbooks. On the 1st of January 1999 the euro became an accepted currency through participating nations in Europe. As the single currency develops, and as the euro becomes better known in the UK, the arguments will continue. What follows is a brief summary. A suggested practical assignment is to research this topic further for yourself.

The main arguments for the single currency are that it:

1.　reduces transaction costs (the cost of changing £ to DM and so on)

2.　reduces exchange rate uncertainty

3.　increases trade and investment between the UK and Europe

4.　stops the fall in inward investment

5.　ensures not only low interest rates but also low inflation (under the control of the European Central Bank).

6.　ensures greater integration in Europe.

The arguments against a single currency

1.　EMU (European monetary union) will fail. Unemployment will rise.

2.　High European interest rates will be needed to quell inflation (or the expectation of it) in particular geographical areas.

3.　Rising economic inequality.

4. Loss of political, economic and legal independence for the UK.

5. To reduce economic inequalities there will have to be fiscal transfers – possible outgoing of funds from the UK.

6. The initial cost to retailers of changing cash tills to accept payment in euros.

The common fisheries policy

Some 500,000 people are employed in fisheries across the EU. The purpose of the common fisheries policy is to:

(a) manage (conserve) EU fish stocks
(b) balance the interests of member states with fishing industries.

There are six key issues:

▶ *Conservation of fish stocks* – Fish stock must be protected. If too many are caught now then supplies in the future will diminish to the point where economic fishing is no longer viable. Member states agree on 'total allowable catches' (TACs) which impose a limit on the output of the fleets. Secondly, the CFP restricts the capacity of the fleet and/or its fishing effort. Technical measures are set by the Council to avoid catches of immature fish. These include minimum net mesh sizes, closed areas and seasons, and minimum landing sizes.

▶ *Discards (fish thrown back)* – These represent a misallocation of resources and a waste.

▶ *Restructuring the fishing industry* – Multi-annual guidance programmes (MAGPs) are set for each member state. These fix objectives to ensure that the fishing efforts of the EU fleets match the available resources.

▶ *Community financial aid to the UK* – The total amount of assistance approved for the period 1994-1999 was 123.62 million euros (about £80 million).

▶ *The environment* – Do fishing gear and activities have an adverse impact?

▶ *Quota-hopping* – This term describes vessels which are owned in one member state, but which fish on the quotas allocated to another member state.

In 1988 the Conservative government passed laws to try and prevent the 'exploitation' of quotas. Spanish companies such as Factortame Ltd and almost 100 other Spanish fishing companies brought a case against the British government. They claimed for losses incurred while their ships were laid up between 1988-1991. The law lords found in favour of the Spanish company, and Britain will have to pay compensation estimated at £100m. The Conservatives were trying to protect British fishing communities but the way in which they did this was illegal. The effect was to discriminate against Spanish nationals, thereby flouting one of the most basic principles of European law.

The Merchant Shipping Act

The British taxpayer will pay for the action of the Conservative government, which passed the Merchant Shipping Act. This UK law, which took effect in 1988, prevented Spanish-owned ships from fishing against UK quotas, or 'quota-hopping'. While there must be no discrimination on the grounds of nationality, an economic link must exist between such vessels and the quota-holding member state. Following the Icelandic cod war in the 1970s, Spanish fishing companies started buying UK-registered ships. The European Court of Justice overturned the Merchant Shipping Act on the grounds that it conflicted with European law on discrimination.

By enacting the Merchant Shipping Act and banning Spanish ships, the UK government has been in breach of EU law on discrimination. This breach has been of such seriousness, said the law lords, that compensation for the Spanish fishermen was payable.

Tutorial: helping you learn

Progress questions

1. Outline one argument against the single currency.

2. What is a 'transaction cost'?

3. Why did the law lords rule in favour of Spanish fishermen?

Discussion points

1. Is the single currency just an economic measure, just a political measure or neither?

2. Staying outside the Euro seems to have attracted inward investment to the UK. What categories of business may be deterred from investing in the UK as long as it stays outside of the Euro. Are the arguments 'for' Europe, weakening?

Practical assignments

1. Fully evaluate the arguments for and against the single currency. Sort out the myths from the reality. These web sites may help:

Single currency	http://www.new-europe.co.uk/
Pro-Europe	http://www.euromove.org.uk/
Against Europe	http://www.bfors.com/ and http://www.ft.com/emu

2. Much was written about Labour's five economic tests that had to be met before they urged joining Europe upon the British electorate. Outline the contents of each 'test' and assess whether the UK has reached the targets set.

Study/revision tip

Next time you go abroad to Europe, think how much you lose in exchanging your currency.

23

Decision Making

One-minute summary – Decisions are made every day in business: whether to expand or contract the business, whether to employ extra workers or sub-contract, what price to charge for a product. Decisions may be short-term or long-term, tactical or strategic. The level of decision determines who makes it. Whatever the decision, all decision-making goes through certain stages. In this chapter we will discuss:

▶ stages in the decision-making process
▶ examples of decisions
▶ types of decision

Stages in the decision-making process

Identifying the objectives
In his pre-Budget report Chancellor Gordon Brown stated:

'Our objectives are:
(a) Britain will raise its productivity faster than its competitors, as we close the productivity gap.
(b) A higher percentage of people in employment than ever before.
(c) A majority of Britain's school and college leavers to go on to higher education for the first time.
(d) Child poverty to be reduced by half, on the way to the Government's 20 year target to end child poverty.' (Source: *Pre-Budget Report* 9.11.99.)

With the objectives set, it is hoped that the workforce (in this context, the whole country) will unite behind a common purpose.

Defining the problem

This identifies the constraints on achieving the objective. Suppose a business has as an objective to increase its profits by 10% a year. One constraint could be the low productivity of the workforce. The problem would therefore be the *cause* of the low productivity. By identifying the cause, a solution may be found. Typical causes of low productivity include:

1. lack of skills required
2. old machinery – operating below the required level of output
3. lack of motivation by the workforce
4. poor organisation – bottlenecks often appearing in production
5. lateness of deliveries by suppliers resulting in a high degree of idle time.

Gathering information and ideas

In order to resolve the problem and/or achieve the objective, information may be needed. Thus in the case of the Chancellor's statement, to achieve the increase in productivity he would need information on:

(a) Numbers of people attending higher education, as productivity depends in part on the skills of the workers. The more people attend higher education, the more highly skilled the workforce is likely to be.

(b) Population demographics to identify where to target resources. For example, if one region has a high percentage of 16–18 year olds, that area needs more educational facilities.

(c) Range of courses available to identify whether the available courses fit the needs of business.

(d) Levels of investment.

(e) Type of investment.

(f) Full analysis of countries with higher productivity than in the UK.

Evaluating ideas and information

This would include any caveats on the accuracy of the information gathered, and how current the figures are. Each possible course of action needs to be assessed in both quantitative and qualitative terms. For example, if more finance is found for investment, is there an opportunity cost? What are the risks involved?

Making the decision

The final decision must take into account its probable impact. Will it lead to redundancies? Will further money have to be borrowed, and if so at what cost? Are government sources of finance available? How committed will the workforce be to this decision? Are contingency plans available, should unforeseen circumstances call for a change of plan?

Communicating the decision

All the interested parties should now have the decision communicated to them. The draft proposals could be circulated as a 'pre-decision' first, for comments. Perhaps others will spot errors or unrealistic assumptions. Maybe the decision will be made based on information that was later proved to be incorrect.

By involving others in the decision-making – or at least asking for feedback on the proposed decision – the manager will find it easier to implement the decision. For example, if the final conclusion is to make 10% of the workforce redundant, union resistance will be minimised if the unions have formed part of the decision-making team.

Evaluating the results

Having made the decision, it is not enough just to sit back and wait for results. There should be re-evaluation at every stage of the implementation process. For example, if it has been decided to launch a product nationally, the business will want daily sales figures to assess whether extra steps should be taken to ensure that targets are being reached.

Obtaining post-decision feedback

The final stage is to write a full report on the steps leading to the decision. This will be useful later if the decision appears to have been correct – or incorrect. By keeping a record, management can learn from their successes/mistakes.

Examples of decisions

Example 1 – Should price be cut?
Consider:

1. estimated price sensitivity of the market
2. likely reaction of competitors
3. percentage of total sales represented by the one product
4. likely reaction from those in the distribution chain
5. current sales, stocks and contribution
6. current mark-up on the product
7. stage of the product life cycle that the product appears to be in
8. effect – if any – on other products in the product mix
9. reasons for even considering this strategy
10. what other strategies are available

Example 2 – Should 5% of the workforce be made redundant?
Consider:

1. likely effect on industrial relations
2. costs involved
3. absolute number of workers involved
4. trade union reaction
5. reason for the redundancies
6. a short or long term solution – if so, to what problem?
7. legal formalities in making workers redundant
8. how will they be selected?

The decision-making process is one of the central themes in Business Studies. It is vital that all factors – and all parties – are considered before taking a decision that may have far-reaching effects.

Types of decision

Strategic decisions

A strategic decision is one that aims long-term. It is likely to have an impact on all departments since it will concern the objectives of the organisation as a whole, not just one particular section. Such decisions are made by the top management of the organisation. For instance, in a limited company this would be the board of directors.

Tactical decisions

A tactical decision is one that aims medium-term. An example would be to introduce new machinery to modify the product as sales have been falling. Such decisions may be made by the board of directors, but could also be delegated to operational or middle management.

Operational decisions

These are short-term decisions. Supervisory staff can make them freely as part of their day to day running of the business deciding which supplier to use for a particular product, for example.

▶ *Note* – strategic decisions may be known as policy decisions; tactical decisions are also known as management decisions; operational decisions are broadly administrative decisions. The key point is that operational decisions contribute to tactics, which in turn contribute to strategy.

Tutorial: helping you learn

Progress questions

1. What are the stages in the decision-making process?

2. If a business decides to change price in response to the actions of a competitor, is that a strategic or tactical decision?

3. Give an example of a tactical decision made by the marketing department.

4. Define 'purchasing strategy'.

Discussion point
Is there a trade-off between expanding a business, and acting in the interests of society as a whole? A company may face divided loyalties to its various stakeholders – shareholders, suppliers, trade unions, employees, competitors, retailers, and customers. Which stakeholders should take priority, and why?

Practical assignments
1. Outline the main strategic, tactical and operational decisions behind the growth of Manchester United plc. (Note: This question is *not* just about football strategy!)

2. Pick seven recent news articles, using the web site below. For each company identify one major decision taken by the company during the last 4 weeks. What considerations would have been taken into account before the decision was made?
    http://news.bbc.co.uk/hi/english/business/default.stm

3. Decisions may be short-term or long-term. Which parties would be involved in making the following decisions in a supermarket chain?

    (a) price charged
    (b) recruitment programmes
    (c) location for expansion

Study/revision tip
One way of remembering decision-making is to take a football analogy. The strategy of a team may be to win the league; the tactics during a football game may be to attack; the operational decisions are making sure everyone is warmed up before the match.

24

Internal and External Business Environments

One-minute summary – There are four main functions/departments in a business: Production, Marketing, Finance and Personnel. Within these functions there may be others, such as purchasing, research & development, quality control, public relations and wages. One of the main themes of business studies is the interaction between the external environment and a business. If we think of the business in terms of these functions, we can assess the impact of the environment far more easily. In this chapter we will discuss:

▶ the internal environment
▶ the external environment
▶ the application of the external environment on the internal

The internal environment

The internal environment is comprised of the four main departments in a business: Finance, Production, Marketing, and Personnel.

The Finance department

The Finance department carries out a number of different functions. These typically include:

1. The preparation of final accounts. These comprise a balance sheet, a trading and profit and loss account, and a cash statement. See chapter 9 for further information.

2. Raising finance – short, medium and long-term finance.

3. Allocating expenditure. For this, budgets are created. The most important of these is the sales budget, since it is from projected income that expenditure is allocated.

4. Financial analysis. This includes ratio analysis, that is the financial assessment of the business's own performance and measuring it against the performance of other businesses.

5. Investment appraisal, in other words assessing the likely return on investment in a new product/new machine/promotion scheme.

6. Improving cash flow. This could include debt factoring (selling of debtors' debts to a third party), and the sale and leaseback of the firm's assets.

7. Costing. This may include variance analysis. It could also include appraising various production initiatives such as the costing of production of a particular product.

The Personnel department
This department deals with the following:

1. Wage negotiations with trade unions.

2. Job evaluation – assessing the worth of a particular job to the business. On the basis of this, a wage band may be determined for the job-holder.

3. Recruitment – including advertising, interview and selection.

4. Training – including on-job and off-job.

5. Dismissal – the sacking of a job-holder.

6. Redundancy programmes – the removal of the job and the dismissal or redeployment of the worker.

7. Job analysis – the assessment of the key components of the job. This may be done through observation, interview, looking at previous research, work diary (by the job-holder) or even members of the Personnel department doing the job themselves for a period.

8. Motivation schemes. This could include setting up and managing performance incentives, such as productivity bonuses and merit awards. Also, there could be general schemes such as the improvement of working conditions and regular performance appraisals with the workers.

The Production department
The activities of the production department would typically include:

1. production
2. quality control
3. stock control
4. sourcing supplies – supplier evaluation and the placing of orders
5. sampling of products to ensure that quality standards were complied with.

The Marketing department
Marketing is the 'management process responsible for identifying, anticipating and satisfying consumers wants and needs profitably' (the Chartered Institute of Marketing). Marketing activities include:

1. advertising
2. branding
3. packaging
4. promotion
5. pricing
6. market research
7. after sales service
8. new product development
9. publicity

10. channel of distribution – manufacturer, wholesaler, retailer, and consumer.

Summary
The above list of departmental functions is not a definitive one. It simply identifies the main core activities carried out by each function within a business.

The external environment

The external environment may be categorised into five 'sub-environments':

Economic
This includes government policies towards inflation, unemployment, economic growth and the balance of payments. The use of tools such as interest rates and taxation to control demand or stimulate supply (see chapter 8).

Political
This includes privatisation policy, policy towards European integration, and also policies about the allocation of government revenue by public expenditure. Politics also affect the legislation passed and, through grants, may stimulate the growth of technology.

Social
The social environment affects people's attitudes to work, leisure, consumption (type of goods) crime and education. The social environment may also include the ecological environment and encompasses the activities of pressure groups to prevent or highlight pollution.

Legal
The legal environment comprises national consumer, employment and business law. On a wider basis, it also includes European directives that will impact on businesses and consumers in the UK.

Technological

The technological environment affects the product, the production process, staffing levels and communication.

▶ *Note* – These environments are not mutually exclusive. Pressure groups, for example, could be viewed in both social and political categories; and allocation of government expenditure covers both political and economic spheres.

The application of the external to the internal environment

A worked example follows. Please note that this is not an essay plan, merely a list of items that may be included in an *'impact on a business of ...'* type of question. Consider this example:

> *If the Bank of England raises interest rates in a bid to reduce inflationary pressure, how might this interest rate rise affect a business?*

Worked example

Marketing
A fall in demand, thereby causing a fall in price. The business may increase advertising to compensate. It may also reduce the number of products available and concentrate on its best sellers. The business may also seek fresh markets overseas.

Production
In the short run, stocks may increase since it will take time for production to adjust. Production may move from mass to batch. Some products may be withdrawn.

Personnel
With the fall in demand, some workers may have to be made redundant. Jobs may be amalgamated. Workers may become demotivated as a result of job insecurity. Trade unions will seek assurances from management. Wage demands are unlikely to be met.

Finance
If sales fall, then cash flow will also fall. It would be an unwise moment to raise money by issuing new shares, but the costs of loans is also likely to increase. Savings must be made and cost-cutting measures taken such as changing suppliers and/or reducing the size of the workforce.

▶ *Key point* – Notice that a number of points were highlighted through looking at the various departments and their activities. Realising how the external environment impacts on a business is a key theme in Business Studies. The impact of interest rates could be further explored; consider how a rise in interest rates might affect unemployment (and so the business) and exchange rates (and thus an import/export business).

Tutorial: helping you learn

Progress questions
1. What are the four main departments in a business?
2. What is in the economic external environment?
3. Why might the Bank of England raise interest rates?

Discussion point
The worked example question above shows how the external environment affects a business. How do the activities of each department affect each other? For example, if Marketing decides to drop the price for a product, how might that affect the Personnel, Production and Finance departments?

Practical assignments
1. In his pre-Budget report of 9th November 1999, Chancellor Gordon Brown outlined the current state of the economy. Taking each function of a business, explain how the current state of the economy might influence business decisions. Carry out this activity for a business making a variety of products, some of which are exported. The pre-Budget report can be found here on the internet:

http://news.bbc.co.uk/hi/english/uk-politics/newsid-506000/
506516.stm

2. Online share dealing is on the increase. This has led to an increase in sites offering information about firms and other stockbroking advice. In what ways if at all might government legislate to avoid fraud committed by these online service providers? Apart from Internet facilities (chat rooms, message boards) what other factors may affect share prices?

http://news.bbc.co.uk/hi/english/business/newsid_613000/
613100.stm

3. In the late 1990s fears were voiced about the impact of the Social Chapter. Outline how the Social Chapter affects business and evaluate whether fears expressed were justified.

http://www.telegraph.co.uk:80/et?ac=000696345546861&rtmo
=022JNGbq &atmo=99999999&pg=/et/97/6/9/cins09.html.

Study/revision tip
The internal environment may be summarised as Personnel, Production, Finance and Marketing. The external environment includes economic, social, legal, technological and political. Understanding how the internal and the external environment interact is the key to understanding Business Studies.

25

Taking the Examination

One-minute summary – This Studymate is designed to help students preparing for a wide variety of Business Studies examinations. Such examinations test the student's understanding of business principles, in particular decision-making and how the internal and external business environments interact with each other. The format of examination papers may be comprehension, case study, report, essay, numerical, or short answer. In this chapter we will discuss:

▶ numerical questions
▶ comprehension questions
▶ case study questions
▶ essay questions

Numerical questions

Business Studies examinations may test:

1. moving averages
2. correlation
3. ratio analysis
4. discounted cash flow
5. break-even
6. variance analysis
7. budgets
8. elasticity.

Approaches to numerical questions

▶ *Mental arithmetic* – Brush up on your mental arithmetic! It is surprising how many Business Studies A-level students are seemingly unable to calculate percentages. Equally surprising is their inability to estimate answers. Thus when they use their calculator, input mistakes leading to incorrect answers which may not be spotted. A mental calculation of 20 x 196 should tell you that the answer is roughly 4,000, so a calculator-based answer that is in tens of thousands should immediately be rejected.

▶ *Double-check* – Usually there is time to double-check your calculations, so always try and do this. The 'OFR' (own figure rule) means that interpretations that are correct but are based on incorrect figures, will still be awarded marks – but how much better to get it right in the first place.

▶ *Formats and formulae* – Many numerical questions are based on formulae. Therefore, make absolutely sure that you learn formulae just as you would learn vocabulary. Ratio analysis, elasticity and variance analysis – all these rely on the interpretation of formula-based calculations. A cash budget, balance sheet and trial balance rely on format. Formats and formulae – commit them to memory.

▶ *Relevance* – Sometimes tables of figures are given and you are asked to interpret and apply them (as in the case of Paper 3 for AEB Business Studies). Remember, not *all* the figures may be relevant to the question asked. One of the skills required is the ability to distinguish relevant information from that which is not.

▶ *Trends* – Look for trends in figures. For example, when using index numbers and asked to comment on a graph, look for the overall trend, the high point and the low point. It will not be necessary to comment on every figure but to use particular points as examples for the comments made. Thus there is no need to write: 'In 1996 the figure was 34 and 1997, 45 and 1998 56', since anyone can just copy out a few figures. Far better to write: 'During the periods 1996-8 the figures rose 22 points. The high point was 56 in 1998'.

Comprehension questions

Perhaps the major mistake made by candidates when tackling comprehension questions, is to run out of time. Too long is spent reading and re-reading the text in the vain search for the 'hidden' answer.

More often than not, the answer to the question is not in the actual text. Rather, the candidates are required to comment using their own knowledge. Time is lost, and then the final section to the question – usually the one with the highest marks – is omitted or rushed.

Case Study questions

Many students find case studies the hardest part of the overall examination. The information is fictitious and so candidates are asked to apply their knowledge in one or a series of situations. Often students may only take the case study once unlike other modules, and so the first sitting is also the last. A method favoured by many teachers is as follows:

▶ *Glance through* – Scan through all the questions before reading the case study. Often the first question will ask you to 'explain/ define' terms in the case study. You may be able to deduce the meaning from the context. Being aware that certain terms are significant while reading the case study should help your understanding.

▶ *Highlight* – When reading through the case study, use a highlighter pen to code the key areas. This will make quick reference that much easier.

▶ *Numbers* – Pay particular attention to any numerical information. Even if questions are not asked directly about the figures, you may need to quote them as examples of increased turnover, responsiveness of demand to price, etc.

▶ *Testing your skills* – The case study is designed to test you on some important skills: social, communication, creativity, application, and analytical. You can practise these skills by doing other case studies throughout your course of study.

Examiner's comment

'Where students go wrong is, first, in ignoring the theoretical studies undertaken during the course and second, in ignoring the interrelationship between case study material and other areas of the syllabus ...' (Source:

Bruce Jewell, Chief Examiner for A-level Business Studies. in *An Integrated Approach to Business Studies*).

Essay questions

When you read the question, make sure that your answer is *not* a pre-planned essay you committed to memory before the examination. Relevance is the key. Often questions ask candidates to 'examine the impact on a business of ...' In this case, to elicit the points, think in terms of the four departments: Production, Personnel, Marketing and Finance. Mention the impact on all of them if relevant.

The Finance department, for example, is involved in wages, costing, producing accounts, cashflow planning, budgeting, breakeven analysis, financial analysis and raising finance. Thus the 'impact on a business' of a rise in unemployment may be analysed in terms of (for Finance) a fall in cashflow: wages fall, prices fall, profits fall, and sales revenue falls, but costs may also fall.

Keeping in mind the departments in a business, try out the following questions:

Typical essay questions
Examine the impact on a business of:

1. the activities of pressure groups
2. a rise in interest rates
3. a fall in the exchange rate
4. government policies to reduce inflation
5. trade union activity – a change in employment legislation
6. joining the single European currency.

Make sure also when writing your essay that:

(a) You define all key terms.
(b) There is a logic and structure to your essay.
(c) Each sentence really is a sentence, not just a series of points.
(d) Your answer is planned and the question is analysed.

▶ *Tip* – 'All essays have the same answer. With few exceptions, A-level essay questions can be answered in two words: 'It depends' The cause or solution to a business problem or opportunity usually depends upon a series of factors, such as the company's objectives and the internal and external constraints it faces ...' (Source: *Business Studies* by Marcouse and others, page 617.)

Tutorial: helping you learn

Progress questions

1. In what sense do all essays have the same answer?

2. Give examples of two formulae that should be committed to memory.

3. What student skills are tested by a case study question?

Discussion point

How important is it to read newspapers when you are preparing for numerical and comprehension questions?

Practical assignment
Define the following terms:

(a) analyse
(b) analysis
(c) assess
(d) define
(e) describe
(f) discuss
(g) evaluate
(h) examine
(i) explain
(j) illustrate
(k) outline

Study/revision tip

When essay-writing, think in terms of departments and their functions as together representing 'a business'. The 'impact on a business' is the impact upon each and all of the departments.

Glossary of Terms

advertising elasticity of demand This measures how demand responds to a change in advertising expenditure.

aggregate demand The total spending on goods and services made within a particular country.

Balance of Payments A summary record of all the financial transactions between one country and the rest of the world.

balance sheet A formal statement of all the assets and liabilities of an organisation on a specified date.

black market A market in which goods and services are traded through unofficial, undeclared or illegal channels. This commonly happens when prices are fixed and there is excess demand.

break-even A firm breaks even when it makes neither a profit nor a loss. The break-even point on a graph is where sales revenue = total cost. An important element in break-even is 'contribution' (selling price – variable cost) as break-even may be calculated as the point where total contribution covers fixed costs.

capital Money invested in the business from shareholders (share capital) or from lenders (loan capital). Capital may also refer to fixed assets such as buildings or machinery.

cashflow The net amount of cash flowing into and out of a business during a specified period.

cost push inflation The supply curve shifts to the left. This indicates a rise in costs and an unwillingness of firms to supply goods at the previous prices. See also demand-pull inflation.

critical path analysis An aspect of network analysis, used to allocate time and resources in the most efficient way.

cross-elasticity of demand This measures how the price change of one good affects the demand for another.

debtor Someone who owes money to a business, such as a customer who has been supplied on credit.

deficit A shortfall of money.

deflation A decrease in demand for products and services, and a consequent fall in prices. See inflation.

demand The desire to own a good or a service. Effective demand is where the demand may be met as there are sufficient funds to make the purchase. Potential demand is where the finances exist to make the purchase but the desire to buy is not there. This type of buyer may be attracted by advertisements. Latent demand is where the desire to buy is there but there are insufficient funds. This type of buyer may be attracted by credit availability.

demand curve A graph which shows how many people will buy ('demand') a particular product, and how this demand changes if the customer knows that the price has risen.

demand-pull inflation If the demand curve shifts to the right, there is said to be demand-pull inflation. See also cost-push inflation.

devaluation A reduction in the rate of exchange of a currency.

directive A law prepared within the European Union that must be adopted by each member state in its own parliament.

discount A reduction in the normal price charged.

economic price The lowest price that may be charged for a product or service if the costs are to be covered.

elasticity The responsiveness of aspects of business to changes in the economy and the market place.

elasticity of supply This measures the responsiveness of supply to a change in price.

equilibrium Exactly equal, in balance.

exchange rate The value of one currency in terms of another; the price at which one currency can be exchanged for another in the foreign exchange market.

exports Goods or services sold to markets overseas.

fiscal Relating to matters of taxation.

frictional unemployment The number of people who are unemployed only in the sense that they are between jobs.

growth An increase in output in the economy.

imports Goods or services purchased from overseas.

import controls Government measures to discourage the import of foreign goods and services. These measures may include quotas, subsidies for home-produced goods, embargoes and tariffs.

income elasticity of demand Measures how demand responds to a change in income.

inflation A sustained increase in the general price level.

inward investment Investment in a country by a firm from overseas.

liquidity The measure of a company's ability to pay its debts as they fall due. A company with no ready cash is said to be illiquid.

loss leaders Products sold at a price below cost.

marketing According to the British Chartered Institute of Marketing, marketing is: 'The management process responsible for identifying, anticipating and satisfying consumer needs and wants profitably'. Marketing may also be defined as 'the selling of goods that don't come back to the people that do'.

market price The price that people expect to pay.

monetarism A school of economic thought that believes that inflation is caused by increases in the money supply.

money supply There are several possible definitions, but a general definition is the value of all notes and coins in circulation, plus money in credit and deposit accounts in banks.

personal savings ratio The relationship between the savings and disposable income after tax of individuals.

price earnings ratio The market price of a share divided by the earnings per share. For example, if the price is 90p and the earnings per share is 10p, the p/e ratio is 9.

price elasticity of demand Measures how demand responds to a change in price.

product life cycle All products go through the same stages from conception, to introduction (to the market), growth, maturity, saturation through to decline. The product life cycle describes the life of the product as it goes through these stages.

product mix The range of products that a company offers.

recession A drop in national economic output. In the UK it is technically defined as 'two consecutive quarters of negative economic growth'.

strategic decision One that aims long-term.

structural unemployment Unemployment resulting from the decline of a particular industry.

supply The willingness of producers to produce and deliver a range of goods/services. Generally, the higher the price, the more will become available.

tariff A tax on an imported product or service

trade discount A discount offered to people trading in the same sector.

unemployment The number of people out of work. The government technical definition refers to those who are registered as able, available and willing to work at the going wage rate in any suitable job.

working capital The money required by a business to cover its day-to-day running costs such as purchasing materials, paying wages, and extending credit to customers.

Index